Employment law for line managers

Produced and published by:

Collinson Grant
Ryecroft
Aviary Road
Worsley
Manchester
M28 2WF

ISBN 978 0 9564337 1 8

Collinson Grant Limited
33 St James's Square
London
SW1Y 4JS

Telephone: (0) 161 703 5600
E-mail: postmaster@collinsongrant.com

Printed in the United Kingdom using paper produced from sustainable sources.
Design, typesetting and production – Centrix Q2 Limited www.cq2.co.uk

Employment law for line managers

Collinson Grant is a management consultancy that helps to improve the performance of employers in the private sector, in Central Government and in Healthcare. Our work focuses on costs, people and organisation. Our human resources specialists support line and personnel managers in every aspect of managing people, particularly on assignments related to employment law, employee relations and reward. The notes at the back will tell you more about what we do.

www.collinsongrant.com

Contents

1. Introduction and the nature of employment law

1 Introduction and the nature of employment law

Collinson Grant started work in the early 1970s. 'Employment law' only truly became a discrete subject with critical mass in 1971, when the Industrial Relations Act was passed. So, we have grown up with it. The law concerning formal relationships and day-to-day behaviour of employees has been a constant consideration in our work supporting clients. And that means we have seen the shape and content of the subject evolve and we understand how best to work with it. It also goes some way to explaining why, by first publishing The Line Manager's Employment Law as far back as 1978, we wanted to emphasise to managers the importance of employment law to their day-to-day responsibilities.

The legal aspects of employment are, thankfully, not the most important elements in relationships at work, which are also shaped by custom, responsibility and mutual expectation. Traditionally, the law dealt rather with the exceptional situation in which these normal affiliations and behaviours were disrupted and, even today, workplace dialogue rarely revolves around the nuances of the latest statute or judicial pronouncement.

The increasing scope and influence of employment law

An increasing number of rights and duties associated with employment are derived from legislation, often supported by codes of practice. In turn, that has affected the scope and nature of what each party expects of the relationship. Consequently, the law has moved from the wings towards the centre of the stage. Individuals may challenge managers' decisions, and may apply to the employment tribunal for redress. Most of these rights are here to stay, and the institutions of the European Union will continue to demand more. Meanwhile, the law on the responsibilities of trade unions, their officers and their actions in support of their members' interests often changes under political pressure. The relative importance of the two basic strands, individual and collective, as well as that of particular subjects within them, changes. But it cannot be seriously doubted that the overall significance of employment law has grown.

The direct financial cost of infringing legal standards can be over-estimated: perceptions are fuelled by reports in the media of the atypical awards of compensation in some high-profile cases. But, even in more commonplace situations, they can still be high. And the calculation of that particular exposure does not encompass the frequently irrecoverable legal fees, the 'opportunity cost' of managers' lost time, possible damage to employee relations and adverse publicity in the wider community.

Know the law – constraints and opportunities

Line managers must acquire a working knowledge of the basic contours of employment law to avoid elementary errors that might damage the business. They should be able to recognise when specialist advice is necessary. And they might also conclude that the law's standards can help improve motivation and performance by providing a foundation for better communication, greater consistency and a sense of participation.

This book, the successor to The Line Manager's Employment Law, which ran for 25 editions over 30 years, is intended to continue providing that required understanding. It adopts a structure that, although containing some more detail, is largely recognisable from its predecessor. But then, to give the law more life, it adds key points, tips on practical actions or considerations and some illustrations of common errors or misconceptions.

It covers the main provisions of employment law in England, Wales and Scotland. In Northern Ireland the substantive law can be different in some aspects, and you should seek further guidance if you need it. Also, perhaps predictably, the law described in the book generally covers only people working here. However, in view of a decision of the House of Lords, some of the main statutory protections can also be extended to employees of UK entities working overseas. Again, professional advice should be sought on the specific situation.

Employment law – some introductory comments

Scope and foundations

Our employment law is made up of legislation (EU Directives or UK Acts and Regulations) and decisions of the courts (case law). These two sources establish the rules that regulate the relationship between an employer and an employee. Sometimes the law makes a distinction between an 'employee' and a 'worker'. In either case, the relationship is based on the existence of a contract.

Contracts

There are different types of contract. These are discussed in more detail later. Generally, a contract is based on freely-given agreement. So an employer has the freedom to decide with whom to make a contract and with whom not to. There are some restrictions on this freedom. The detailed contents, or 'terms and conditions', of a contract between an employer and employee or worker record the agreed rights and duties, the provisions for terminating the contract and, sometimes, responsibilities (such as confidentiality) after termination.

Minimum rights

Although it is assumed that both parties enter into the contract voluntarily, legislation establishes minimum rights and standards that apply to the relationship. These override the contract, even if it does not mention them, or says that some or all of them do not apply, or specifies inferior provisions.

So, contractual provisions will only be effective if they at least match, or improve on, the equivalent statutory rules. They will be ineffective, and unenforceable, if they attempt to lessen or avoid the statutory provisions. Where a subject is not directly regulated by legislation, the parties (although usually the employer) may specify whatever terms they wish, provided that this does not result in an agreement to do something illegal.

How are employment rights and duties enforced?

Statutory rights and duties are enforced through the employment tribunal system. Employment tribunals can also deal with some contractual claims that are not established by legislation. Otherwise, contractual claims are heard by the County Court or High Court.

2. Employees – establishing who they are

2 Employees – establishing who they are

Many statutory rights at work are only available to 'employees' who work under a 'contract of employment' and are not available to other providers of work or services who operate as independent contractors under a 'contract for services'. For this reason, it can become necessary to determine whether someone is (or was) an employee or some other type of work provider. This may also be important to determine who should pay income tax and National Insurance Contributions.

Is someone an employee or not?

The main questions to be considered are:

- Who has control over how the work is done?
- To what extent is the person integrated into the structure of the organisation? For example, is he or she subject to the employer's disciplinary procedure?
- Who provides the equipment or materials necessary to do the work?
- Must the work be done personally, or may it be delegated to someone else?
- Is there 'mutuality of obligation' (an obligation on the employer to provide work and an obligation on the employee to do the work)?
- How are payments processed and how are they treated for tax and National Insurance?
- Does the person have access to benefits, such as sick pay and pension?
- Are there restrictions on the person's freedom to work for others?

Workers

Some workplace rights are available to 'workers'. A worker is defined more widely than an employee. It includes people who are technically self-employed but who are nevertheless obliged to perform work personally. This could include an independent contractor.

Someone who is neither a worker nor an employee is not covered by statutory employment rights. Such people are regarded as being 'in business on their own account'. The distinction between workers and people in business on their own account is that workers have an obligation of personal performance, that is, to do the work themselves.

Casual workers

Casual workers, which include intermittent, bank and seasonal staff, often operate under short-term contracts of employment, each lasting for the brief period they are engaged to work. If they have been engaged to work with sufficient frequency, they may also be able to argue that their overall relationship with the work-provider spanning all the separate, short-term periods of work is one of a 'global' or 'umbrella' contract of employment (on the grounds that the regular provision of work and agreement to do it create a 'mutuality of obligation'). If this is the case, continuous service (important for some statutory rights) can be calculated to include even the weeks that fell between the discrete periods of actual work.

Conflicting terms and practice

Even if a contract contains terms associated only with a certain status (generally, 'self-employment'), a court or tribunal can look behind it to examine the way the relationship actually operates, or did operate, and, if that points to another status (generally, 'employment'), the court or tribunal can ignore the words of the contract.

Agency temps (workers hired out by 'employment businesses')

An 'employment business' (often known as an employment agency) may directly employ people seeking work under a contract of employment and supply them temporarily to work for, and be controlled by, a hiring organisation. Or the person the agency supplies works under a contract for services and so is not regarded as an employee of the agency. The agency must confirm to both the work-seeker and the hirer in writing whether the worker is its employee or is working under a contract for services.

Although it is unlikely, a tribunal could decide that someone hired out by an employment business had, through a lengthy relationship and 'mutuality of obligation', an implied contract of employment with the hirer.

Draft regulations proposed for implementation in 2011 would give hired-out workers the same terms and conditions as the hirer's own employees after 12 weeks' engagement.

Use of temporary labour during industrial action

Legislation prohibits an employment business from knowingly supplying a worker (a) to do the work of one of the hirer's employees if that employee is participating in official industrial action, or (b) to do the job of another employee who has been transferred to cover for the employee who is on strike.

3. The contract

3 The contract

Restrictions on an employer's freedom to make (or not make) a contract

There are three main types of statutory restriction:

Discrimination

The first restriction is laws against discriminating on grounds of sex, sexual orientation, race, religion or belief, disability and age.

Issues of union membership

The second restriction is concerned with trade union membership. It is unlawful to refuse employment on grounds that a person:

- is, or is not, a member of a trade union
- will not agree to become, to cease to be, to remain or to refuse to be a member of a union
- will not agree to make payments or have deductions made from pay for not being a member of a trade union.

Compensation for a successful complaint to an employment tribunal can be up to £65,300.

It is proposed to introduce legislation in 2010 to prohibit the making and use of 'blacklists' of trade unionists.

Employment of illegal immigrants

The third restriction is concerned with legislation on illegal immigrants. For employment that started on or before 28th February 2008, it is a criminal offence to employ a migrant aged 16 or over who does not have permission to live or work in the UK. The offence carries a fine of up to £5,000.

For employment that started after 28th February 2008, there are two types of offence:

- *negligently employing an illegal immigrant.* This carries a fine of up to £10,000. It is a possible defence if the employer conducted a pre-employment check of one or more specified documents (the legislation provides lists of what are acceptable documents) that prove the person's right to work in the UK, either indefinitely or for a limited period. However, if it is for a limited period, any defence derived from the pre-employment check will lapse after 12 months, unless further checks have been made.

  If TUPE (see Chapter 9) applies, the incoming employer has 28 days to comply with the checking requirements for this offence.

- *knowingly employing an illegal immigrant.* This offence carries a prison term of up to two years and/or an unlimited fine.

In both of the above cases it is not just the employing company that faces prosecution. Its directors, managers and other senior officers can also be prosecuted if the offence is committed with their consent or collusion, or because of their neglect.

It is a defence to show that, before recruitment, the employee produced a document specified in the legislation that appeared to relate to him or her and the employer kept it or took a copy of it. This defence applies even if the document turns out to be fraudulent, unless the employer knew that it would be illegal to employ the person.

Creation of contract and consequences

A contract of employment (and a contract for services) is formed as soon as a candidate accepts an offer of employment from an employer. However, a candidate's acceptance will have no effect if the employer has communicated withdrawal of the offer before that acceptance is received.

Once a contract is formed, the employee (or worker) and the employer are bound by its terms. A basic contract will be created even before the work has started or payment has been made for it. This contract could be terminated before the person starts work. If, as sometimes happens, an employer terminates the contract without notice (often saying, incorrectly, that the offer is being withdrawn) the amount of damages is normally pay for the contractual notice period.

Common misconception (1)

'...the expiry of a limited-term contract cannot have any legal consequences'

It can. Expiry without renewal amounts to a dismissal. And, although the employer generally has a head start in defending any allegation of unfair dismissal (the expiry was agreed at the outset and is often because there is no more work), there can be problems.

Difficulties can arise if a particular employee was not offered continuation in the post under another contract (and someone else was recruited) because of some unacceptable reason. Or, it could be that, although the particular post lapsed with the expiry of the contract, there was alternative employment that was not properly considered.

In any event, there is always the need for an employer to notify (or remind) the employee of the prospect that employment will end and to apply an appropriate pre-termination procedure.

Recording terms

To reduce the likelihood of and scope for misunderstanding or dispute, written contracts or a written record of key provisions are desirable.

The written statement of employment particulars

It is a statutory requirement to provide an employee with this statement within two months of starting work. The statement is not, strictly, the contract of employment – it is merely evidence of the main terms of the contract. However, employers often include the subjects required by law in a broader, formal contract of employment. This also contains provisions on other matters (for example company cars, other benefits, and restrictions on post-termination activities).

What the statement of employment particulars must contain:

1 date(s) when employment and continuous employment began
2 scale or rate of remuneration or method of its calculation
3 intervals at which remuneration is paid
4 hours of work
5 holiday entitlement and arrangements
6 place of work or, if various places of work are contemplated, an indication of that and the employer's address
7 job title or brief description of the work
8 sickness and pension arrangements
9 disciplinary rules and procedure, and procedures for dismissal
10 grievance procedure
11 particulars of any collective agreements directly affecting terms and conditions or, if none, a statement to that effect. Where there is such a collective agreement, its terms, for example on pay, become incorporated into the employee's contractual terms)
12 entitlement to notice
13 expiry date of a fixed-term contract or the expected duration of any other temporary contract
14 if the employee is required to work outside the UK for more than one month, the duration of that period, any additional remuneration or benefits and any terms and conditions about return to the UK.

Information can be given in instalments and by reference

Employment particulars (1) – (14) may be given in instalments, as long as the employee is provided with all the information within two months of starting.

Points (1) to (7) must, however, be contained in a single document. This is known as the 'principal statement'. Items (8) to (14) may also be in that document, or in a subsequent statement.

For items (8) to (11), it is permitted to make reference to other documents, specifying where those other documents may be found. For item (12), it is permitted to make reference to legislation or a collective agreement with a trade union.

If no information is to be provided under any heading, this must be stated.

If there are changes to the required content

Any change to the required content of the statement must be notified to the employee personally, in writing, within a month of the change. Of course this does not, in itself, mean that the employer has the right to change contractual terms without the employee's consent.

The employee's right to consult the employment tribunal

An employee can apply to the employment tribunal to determine employment particulars. In addition, if an employee succeeds in a claim to the tribunal about a separate right (for example, unfair dismissal) and the tribunal finds that the employer has not complied with the duty to provide particulars, it can award between two and four weeks' pay to the (ex-) employee.

There are four main types of contractual term:

- Express – they have been spelt out and may be written or oral. They have been expressly agreed between the parties and can only be overridden by law. An express term will be void if it attempts to deprive someone of statutory rights.
- Implied – not spelt out, but are either so obvious they do not need recording, or are custom and practice. Or a term can be implied because the conduct of the parties demonstrates that they did agree on a point of the contract, even though they did not formally say so. A court will look at what it presumes to be the real intention of the parties when determining whether there is an implied term.
- Incorporated – from other sources such as a collective agreement, works rules or company handbook. Terminology can be important. In one case (Alexander v Standard Telephones and Cables) the (unsuccessful) claimant's statement of employment terms said the 'basic terms and conditions of [your] employment are in accordance with and subject to the provisions' of the collective agreement. The collective agreement included a redundancy procedure. But the court decided it was not incorporated. The words used were 'the basic terms and conditions' are to be found in the collective agreement. The basic terms were only those required by the statutory principal statement of employment particulars – so the redundancy procedure was not contractual.
- Statutory – derived from provisions of statutes (such as an 'equality clause' inserted by the Equal Pay Act 1970).

Implied terms in a contract

Implied terms exist in every contract. They are not shown in the statement of particulars or a written contract of employment, yet they still place obligations on the employer, the employee, or both. Implied terms are those that are:

- regarded as integral to a personal relationship, such as mutual trust and confidence, or the exercise of reasonable care and skill
- considered so obvious to the relationship that the parties would have included them had they been asked or thought about it
- derived from statutory requirements, for example an 'equality clause'
- based on 'custom and practice'.

The relationship between implied terms and express terms

An implied term in a contract cannot override an express (explicitly stated) term that contradicts it on the same subject (an aspect of pay for example, such as overtime rates). However, implied terms are often about standards of conduct. For example, say a contract contains the express right to put the employee on 'other duties'. It is possible for that right to be exercised in such a harsh or unreasonable way that it amounts to a breach of an implied term (particularly that of trust and confidence).

The importance of trust and confidence

The implied obligation of trust and confidence is so central to employment that any breach of it entitles the injured party to treat the contract as not just breached but also ended. An injured employer will be able to dismiss without notice (as long as a proper investigation takes place and a satisfactory procedure is followed). A wronged employee will be able to resign and be treated as 'constructively' dismissed.

'That's it, I've had enough'

How does one decide whether there has been a 'termination' of a contract?

In many cases, there will be no doubt. The intention of the employer or employee will be quite clear from the natural meaning of the words used in a letter or a conversation. And subsequent behaviour will generally confirm the fact.

But there are situations in which the context and significance of words and/or actions have to be considered more carefully, either by the party to whom they are addressed or by the employment tribunal. Ambiguity of wordings and contradictory messages are often the problem. On other occasions, even combinations of words with a superficially clear meaning merit further evaluation.

For example, in a heated dispute an employee says on leaving, 'That's it, I've had enough'. If the employer takes that utterance literally and proceeds to treat the employee as having resigned, there may be difficulty.

Many of the immediate, post-departure measures that an employer takes (P45, collection of company property, denial of access to the computer system) are the same as those that are taken when there is a dismissal. This means that an overly hasty, unverified or unforgiving response to words spoken by an employee in the heat of the moment can end up as amounting to exclusion by the employer and, effectively, a dismissal.

See Chapter 10 for more information about the termination of contracts.

4. Statutory employment rights – pay, hours and holidays

4 Statutory employment rights – pay, hours and holidays

National minimum wage

A worker (not just an employee) has the right to receive the national minimum wage (NMW) unless he or she is:

- an apprentice aged 18 or still in the first year of apprenticeship
- a student or trainee on work placement
- a voluntary worker
- living in the employer's home, working as part of the family and not paying for subsistence (such as an au pair).

The hourly rates of the NMW are normally adjusted annually.

The hourly rates from October 2009 are:

Standard	£5.80
Ages 18–21 and those aged 22 or over who are in the first six months of a job under an accredited training scheme	£4.83
Ages 16–17	£3.57

How is the hourly rate calculated?

The calculation of the hourly rate (to determine compliance with the NMW) is to divide an employee's total gross pay by the number of hours worked during the 'pay reference period'.

Gross pay includes commission, bonuses, and gratuities paid through the payroll. It excludes payment for overtime, shift premiums, unsocial hours allowances, London weighting, stand-by payments and gratuities received direct from customers.

The pay reference period (PRP) is one month, unless the worker is paid weekly or daily, in which case it is the shorter period. If the work done in one PRP is not actually paid until the next PRP (for example, because payment is made monthly in arrears), the pay can be attributed to the earlier PRP to calculate the hourly rate.

The method for calculating the hourly rate depends on the type of work involved:

- *time work* (payment by the number of hours 'worked', wherever the location). Admissible hours include those on business travel during normal working time and on stand-by or on-call near the workplace (but not at home) and exclude those when the worker is on a rest-break or absent
- *salaried work* (payment in equal instalments through the year for a set basic minimum number of hours). Admissible hours are the same as for time work, except that absences attracting normal pay and rest breaks that form part of basic hours are counted
- *output work* (payment according to the amount of work done, for example the number of items produced or sales made, unless this is classified as time work). Payment must be either for hours worked on business travel plus every hour of actual work, or according to a 'fair piece rate'. A fair piece rate is set at 1.2 times the time taken by an average worker of the employer to earn the NMW. This gives workers who may be below average the opportunity to earn the NMW. The fair piece rate must be notified to the worker in writing
- *unmeasured work* (that is, not 'time work', 'salaried work' or 'output work'). This includes work for which there are no specified hours. Admissible hours are those spent on business travel plus either every hour of actual work or those fixed by a 'daily average agreement'. This is a written agreement made before the start of the pay reference period that it covers, stating the daily average hours the employee is expected to work each day.

Pay records must be kept for 3 years

Records of pay and any daily average agreements must be kept for this period. The worker can make a written request to see personal pay records and to copy them. An employer's refusal of a request, or failure to respond to one, can result in an employment tribunal awarding the worker a sum equal to 80 times the NMW.

How is the minimum rate enforced?

Enforcement of the NMW can be by a worker's application to a court or tribunal, or by HM Revenue and Customs. An employer may be fined up to £5,000 for non-compliance.

A worker has the right not to be subjected to a detriment by their employer for relying on NMW entitlements. A successful complaint to the employment tribunal that the worker has been victimised for doing so can result in compensation.

Itemised pay statement

Employees have the right to receive an itemised statement that sets out gross earnings, net pay, and fixed and variable deductions. An employee can complain to the employment tribunal if no statement has been provided, or if the statement does not refer to an 'unnotified deduction' (a deduction that the employee has not been told about). The tribunal can award compensation up to a maximum of the total unnotified deductions in the 13 weeks up to the complaint being made.

Deductions from pay

Deductions from a worker's 'wages' (this covers salary) are unlawful unless:

- the deduction is allowed by statute (such as National Insurance, tax and court orders)
- the deduction is provided for in the contract or
- the worker has given written consent for the deduction before the deduction was made.

The same restrictions apply to any requirement or demand for a worker to make payments to the employer from his or her 'wages'.

The expression 'wages' includes holiday pay, Statutory Sick Pay (SSP) and Statutory Maternity Pay (SMP) but excludes compensatory severance payments.

A 'deduction' occurs when a worker receives less than the amount that is 'properly payable' according to the contract or any other legal obligation or commitment. So, for example, an employer's non-payment of remuneration for time that a worker spent taking industrial action, whether 'official' or not (see Chapter 14) would not be a 'deduction' – because, subject to certain exceptions, the worker is not entitled to receive pay for time spent absent from work.

Some types of deduction are excluded from the restrictions, including those to reimburse overpayments of pay or expenses.

A worker can complain to the employment tribunal about an unlawful deduction from pay or an unlawful payment demanded by the employer. If a claim is successful, the employer will be ordered to reimburse the employee and will lose the right to recoup the money in the future. The employer may also be required to compensate the employee for any further financial loss suffered because of the unlawful deduction or payment.

In retail, deductions for stock deficiencies or cash shortages are, in any event, limited to 10% (gross) of any single instalment of pay (except for the final one, to which no limit applies).

The deduction of trade union subscriptions from pay by the employer ('check-off') requires the employee's written authorisation before the deduction is made. Otherwise, the deduction is recoverable (from the employer) by complaint to the employment tribunal.

Guarantee payment

An employee is entitled to a guarantee payment for any day on which he or she is temporarily laid off. The payment is based on the 'guaranteed hourly rate'. This is calculated by dividing 'one week's pay' by the contractual number of weekly hours and multiplying the result by the number of hours of work lost on the day in question. The current maximum (from February 2010) guarantee payment is £21.20 per day. The rate is reviewed annually.

An employee's entitlement to guarantee payments is limited to five days in any three-month period (for a normal five-day week). Payment is conditional on:

- the employee having at least one month's continuous employment
- the lay-off not being due to a trade dispute

- the employee not having unreasonably refused to do suitable alternative work
- entitlement not having been exhausted in the previous three months.

An employee can complain to the employment tribunal that a guarantee payment is due. If successful, the tribunal may order the employer to pay the amount due.

There is a possible exemption from the right to a guarantee payment if a collective agreement already makes provision.

The employer's overall liability

Unless an employee's contract clearly allows for lay-off without pay or for short-time working on reduced pay, the employer will be liable to pay the full contractual daily or weekly rate (which will include the statutory guarantee payment). If the employer fails to pay the full contractual rate, it will be in breach of contract and open to claims for unlawful deduction from wages. If the employee resigns to establish 'constructive' dismissal, the employer will be open to claims for unfair dismissal and/or a statutory redundancy payment.

There are separate statutory provisions giving an employee the right to a statutory redundancy payment following a period of short-time working and/or lay-off. These use a different definition of 'lay-off' based on a full week without work.

Pay for medical suspension

If specified health and safety regulations require employees to be suspended from work, they have a right to pay for up to 26 weeks. This provision does not cover absence for 'ordinary' sickness or injury.

Conditions for payment and for enforcement are similar to those for a guarantee payment. An employment tribunal is able to award up to 26 weeks' pay to a successful complainant.

Statutory sick pay

Statutory Sick Pay (SSP) is payable for a maximum of 28 weeks in any period of incapacity for work or linked periods of incapacity. A period of incapacity for work is an absence from work because of illness of at least four days, whether or not these are working days.

Exceptions to this include employees:

- on short contracts of service
- with earnings below the lower earnings limit for National Insurance Contributions
- who are sick within 57 days of being paid certain State benefits, such as sickness benefits and maternity allowances
- who have done no work under the contract of service
- involved in a trade dispute
- who have received the maximum SSP
- working abroad, outside the European Union
- in legal custody.

Responsibility for direct payment (as 'incapacity benefit') is transferred to the Department for Work and Pensions (DWP):

- at the beginning of the incapacity if the employee is excluded as above, or
- following the maximum entitlement to SSP or
- when liability ceases for some other reason, for example when employment ends.

Statutory sick pay (with effect from April 2009)

Normal Weekly Earnings	**Weekly SSP**
Below £95.00	nil
£95.00 or more	£79.15

The payment rates are reviewed every April.

Reimbursement of the employer

This is by deduction from National Insurance Contributions of the full SSP paid during any month in which it exceeds 13% of gross National Insurance Contributions.

The self-employed, unemployed or non-employed (that is, paying Class 2 or 3 Contributions) are not included in the SSP scheme. They claim benefit directly from the DWP from the beginning of the incapacity.

Working hours

Under the Working Time Regulations, an employer should ensure that a worker (employee or contract worker) does not work more than an average of 48 hours per week. The average is normally taken over a 'rolling' 17-week period. All employers are required to keep records that are sufficient to show whether the limits on working time are being complied with.

However, an employee may enter into an 'opt-out' agreement to avoid the 48-hour restriction. This is terminable by a minimum notice of seven days, and a maximum of three months.

There is no 48-hour maximum on weekly working time for those whose work is classified as 'unmeasured'. Examples of these workers are executives/ managers and family workers, such as au pairs.

Night workers

The hours of night workers should be based on an averaged maximum of eight hours per 24 over the 17-week reference period. This does not apply to people whose jobs involve continuity of care or surveillance, although they are entitled to compensatory rest periods.

All night workers have the right to a free health assessment before starting night work and at regular intervals during it. The purpose is to determine whether the person is fit to do night work.

Younger workers

People aged 15 to 18 are subject to an absolute maximum of eight hours' work a day and 40 hours per week.

Road transport

For all road transport workers there is an absolute maximum of 60 hours per week.

Rest periods

Workers are entitled to one daily rest period of 11 hours in a 24-hour period and one weekly rest period of 24 hours in a seven-day period. In addition, they are entitled to one rest break of 20 minutes during any period of six hours or more. However, different rules apply to young workers and for certain categories of night-worker.

Employers can make some amendments to these obligations if they reach a collective agreement with a trade union or a workforce agreement with elected representatives of the employees. The agreement can include changing the reference period for calculating the average working week and the provisions on rest periods.

Enforcement of working hours

An employee has the right not to suffer a detriment for relying on rights under the Working Time Regulations.

Enforcement of the regulations is either by the Health and Safety Executive (with the possibility of prosecution and unlimited fines) or by an employee's claim to the employment tribunal. A tribunal can award compensation that reflects any loss sustained by the employee as a result of the employer breaching the regulations.

Holidays

The Working Time Regulations also deal with minimum holiday entitlement. From April 2009, workers are entitled to a minimum of 28 days' (or 5.6 weeks') paid annual holiday, which can include bank/public holidays. In the year that the worker joined the employer, the entitlement accrues at the rate of one-twelfth per month. Entitlement for part-time workers who work less than five days per week is calculated pro rata. The Regulations do not generally provide for holidays to be carried over into the next holiday year. And payment in lieu of holidays is generally only allowed on termination of employment.

Of course, the contract of employment can improve on the minimum entitlement. Also, different rules (on carrying over, say) can be applied to the amount of holiday above the minimum.

We missed our flight!

An employer may warn an employee that overstaying leave will be regarded as misconduct that may result in dismissal. But if the employee is dismissed, he or she can still complain of unfair dismissal. To succeed at the employment tribunal, the employer would have to show it acted reasonably.

Notification of leave

Most employers have their own rules for notification of holidays. The regulations also provide a formula: an employee must give advance notification of a period that is at least twice the length of the intended holiday. So, if the employee wants to take two weeks' leave then four weeks' notice must be given. If the employer wants to refuse the employee permission to take a period of leave, the notice required to the employee is the length of the period of leave requested (for example, two weeks in advance of a requested fortnight's leave).

Entitlement accrued during absence

People on maternity leave or extended sickness absence will accrue holiday entitlement during these absences and can choose to take paid leave either during the absence (for example, when entitlement to sick pay has expired) or afterwards. This principle is derived from decisions of the European Court of Justice on the interpretation of the Working Time Directive. In particular, the possibility of employees postponing leave until their return creates a potential conflict with the United Kingdom's own prohibition on carrying over leave (see above).

Enforcement of holiday entitlement

An employee can submit a claim to the employment tribunal if leave has been denied, or if leave has been taken but the employee has not received the appropriate payment for it.

Overpayments on holiday pay

Unless there is an agreement between an employer and employee, if the employee takes more than their annual leave entitlement, the employer cannot recover the equivalent amount in salary.

5. Statutory employment rights – family matters

5 Statutory employment rights – family matters

Time off for ante-natal care

A pregnant employee is entitled to paid time off for ante-natal care. The care must be prescribed by a doctor, midwife or health visitor. After the first visit, the employer can ask for documentary evidence of pregnancy and details of appointments.

If an employment tribunal finds that this time off has been unreasonably refused by the employer, it can award pay for the time off concerned.

Suspension on maternity grounds

Under designated health and safety legislation, an employee is entitled to be transferred (on the same terms and conditions of employment) from a job that might affect her health if:

- she is pregnant
- she has recently given birth, and/or
- she is breastfeeding.

If no suitable work is available, she must be suspended on pay for whatever period is medically certified.

Maternity leave

Qualification and scope

No employee may work for the two weeks following the date of childbirth.

An employee is entitled to a maximum of 52 weeks' maternity leave, comprising 26 weeks' 'ordinary maternity leave' and 26 weeks' 'additional maternity leave'.

To qualify for this entitlement, the employee must notify her employer, by the 15th week before her expected week of childbirth, that she is pregnant, the expected week of childbirth and when she wants the leave to start.

The employee may change the starting date of her leave, provided that she tells her employer at least 28 days in advance of the starting date, unless this is not reasonably practicable. If requested, she must provide a medical certificate that shows the expected date of childbirth.

Once the employee has notified the employer of the starting date of her leave, the employer must respond within 28 days telling the employee the date on which she is expected to return to work if she takes her full entitlement to maternity leave.

The employee can choose to start her leave at any time during the eleven weeks before the expected week of confinement. However, leave starts automatically if the employee is absent for a reason related to pregnancy during the four weeks before the expected week of childbirth.

The contract of employment continues during maternity leave and all the employee's contractual benefits, apart from pay, are maintained during the whole of her leave. The leave period also counts as pensionable service.

Contact during maternity leave

Both the employer and employee may contact each other to discuss matters related to work or maternity, provided that the amount or type of contact is reasonable. An employee may do up to ten 'keeping in touch' days, doing agreed work, for an agreed rate of pay, without bringing her maternity leave to an end. The leave period is extended by the number of days worked.

Return to work after maternity leave

The same notice of return requirements apply both to ordinary maternity leave and to additional maternity leave.

If the employee wishes to return before the end of either the ordinary or additional leave, she must give her employer at least eight weeks' notice of the date she wants to return. If she fails to do so, the employer can postpone her return for up to eight weeks after her request was made, as long as this does not delay her return beyond the end of the full 52 weeks' leave.

The employee does not have to give any notice to return on the expiry of either the 26 weeks' ordinary leave or the 52 weeks' full leave.

After ordinary maternity leave, the employee has the right to return to the job she was in before her leave started, with all the rights she had before her leave started. However, after the additional maternity leave, she may return to the same job, unless it is not reasonably practicable, when a suitable alternative job must be offered.

The employee may ask to return to work part-time after maternity leave (see also flexible working below), If the employer refuses such a request without a business justification, the woman may bring a claim for indirect discrimination.

If the employer refuses to allow a woman to return to work after maternity leave, she will be regarded as dismissed and the dismissal will be automatically unfair. This could lead the woman to make a claim to the employment tribunal and to an award of compensation.

If a woman is found to have suffered a detriment because of pregnancy or maternity leave, an employment tribunal can award her unlimited compensation.

A person taken on as a temporary replacement for a woman on maternity leave can be fairly dismissed, as long as the replacement is informed on engagement that the employment will terminate on the return of the other employee from maternity leave.

Statutory maternity pay

To qualify for statutory maternity pay, a woman:

- must have at least 26 weeks' continuous service (irrespective of the number of hours worked) at the start of the 15th week before the expected confinement (the 'qualifying week') and
- must have average weekly gross earnings in the eight weeks up to and including the qualifying week that are at least equal to the National Insurance lower earnings limit (£95.00 from April 2009) and
- be still pregnant at the 11th week before the expected confinement.

The amount of statutory maternity pay is normally 90% of average weekly earnings for each of the first 6 weeks of maternity leave, followed by 33 weeks at the flat rate (£124.80 from April 2010) or 90% of average earnings if that is less. The total of 39 weeks is known as the Maternity Pay Period.

Any pay rise applying to a woman after the start of the period used to calculate statutory maternity pay and before the end of the maternity leave period is taken into account when calculating the amount of statutory maternity pay due.

If the employee is absent for a pregnancy-related reason on or after the beginning of the fourth week before the expected week of confinement, the maternity pay period starts.

Employers are reimbursed for statutory maternity pay. They may deduct 92% of the gross payment of statutory maternity pay from their monthly National Insurance contributions. Small employers (those whose annual National Insurance contributions are £45,000 or less) recover the full amount.

Paternity leave

Qualification and scope

An employee is entitled to two weeks' paternity leave. The leave can be taken as two consecutive weeks or as one week. If only one week is taken, the entitlement to the second week is lost.

The leave must be taken within 56 days of the actual birth of the child, or if the child is born early, within the period from the actual birth up to 56 days after the originally expected week of birth.

Only one period of leave may be taken, irrespective of whether more than one child is born as a result of the same pregnancy.

To qualify for paternity leave, an employee must:

- have, or expect to have, responsibility for the child's upbringing and
- be the biological father of the child, or the mother's husband or partner and
- have worked continuously for the employer for 26 weeks leading into the 15th week before the baby is due.

To take paternity leave, the employee must tell the employer of his intention to take paternity leave by the 15th week before the baby is expected, and also tell the employer:

- the week the baby is due
- whether he wishes to take one or two weeks' leave
- when he wants the leave to start.

The employer can ask the employee to provide a self-certificate as evidence of entitlement to paternity leave. HMRC has a 'model' self-certificate for this purpose.

The employee can change his mind about when he wants leave to start, provided that he tells the employer at least 28 days in advance of the day he wants leave to start (unless this is not reasonably practicable).

The employee's contract of employment remains in existence during paternity leave, except for terms relating to wages or salary.

The employee is entitled to return to the same job after paternity leave.

The employee is protected from suffering a detriment or unfair dismissal for reasons related to taking, or seeking to take, paternity leave. If the employee believes he has been treated unfairly, he can complain to the employment tribunal, irrespective of his length of service.

Additional paternity leave

It is proposed to introduce legislation (that will be in force from April 2010 and will apply to parents of children due from April 2011) enabling eligible fathers to take Additional Paternity Leave. Under the scheme, fathers will be able to take up to 26 weeks' Additional Paternity Leave, once the mother has returned to work, which may be paid if taken during the mother's maternity pay period. Any leave taken after the mother's maternity pay period expires will be unpaid. The earliest date a father will be able to take the leave will be 20 weeks after the child's birth.

Statutory paternity pay

Statutory paternity pay is payable for up to the maximum two weeks' leave at the same rate as applies to statutory maternity pay after the first six weeks (£124.88 from April 2010).

The means of the employer's reimbursement of paternity pay is the same as for statutory maternity pay.

Adoption leave

Qualification and scope

An employee who has been matched with a child for adoption is an 'adopter'. An adopter is entitled to 26 weeks' ordinary adoption leave, followed by 26 weeks' additional adoption leave – a total of 52 weeks' leave, called the Adoption Leave Period.

To qualify for adoption leave, an employee must be newly-matched with a child for adoption by an approved adoption agency and have worked continuously for the employer for 26 weeks leading into the week in which the match with a child for adoption is notified.

Adoption leave (and adoption pay) are not available when a child is not newly-matched for adoption, for example when a step parent or foster parent is adopting a partner's child.

The adopter is required to inform the employer of the intention to take leave within seven days of notification of having been matched with a child for adoption, unless this is not reasonably practicable. The adopter must tell the employer when the child is expected to be placed and when adoption leave is to start.

The employer can ask for evidence of entitlement to adoption leave. In this case, the adopter must provide a 'matching certificate' from the adoption agency. The adopter must then give the employer 28 days' notice of the date the adoption leave is to start.

The employer has 28 days to respond in writing to an employee's notification of leave. The employer must state when the employee is expected to return to work, assuming the full entitlement to leave is taken.

An adopter can change the date on which adoption leave and Statutory Adoption Pay are to start, giving at least 28 days' notice, unless this is not reasonably practicable.

All contractual benefits, apart from pay, are maintained during the adoption leave period.

Contact during adoption leave

Both the employer and employee may contact each other to discuss matters related to work or adoption, provided that the amount or type of contact is reasonable. An employee may do up to ten 'keeping in touch' days, doing agreed work, for an agreed rate of pay, without bringing her adoption leave to an end. The leave period is extended by the number of days worked.

Return to work after adoption leave

If the employee wishes to return before the end of either the ordinary or additional leave, the employee must give the employer at least eight weeks' notice of the date of return. If the employee fails to do so, the employer can postpone the return for up to eight weeks after the request was made, as long as this does not delay the employee's return beyond the end of the full 52 weeks' leave.

The employee does not have to give any notice to return on the expiry of either the 26 weeks' ordinary leave or the 52 weeks' full leave.

If the employer refuses to allow an employee to return to work after adoption leave, the employee will be regarded as dismissed and the dismissal will be automatically unfair. This could lead the employee to make a claim to the employment tribunal and to an award of compensation.

If an employee is found to have suffered a detriment because of adoption or adoption leave, an employment tribunal can award her unlimited compensation.

Statutory adoption pay

Employees whose weekly average gross earnings are at least equal to the National Insurance lower earnings limit (£95.00 from April 2009) are entitled to statutory adoption pay for a continuous period of 39 weeks (provided that the adoption is not disrupted) at the rate of £124.88 (from April 2010), or, if less, 90% of average earnings.

Paternity leave on adoption

An employee is entitled to take two consecutive weeks' paternity leave within 56 days of the child's (or children's) placement.

The provisions governing the conditions that qualify a person to take leave, the notice of intention to take leave, self-certification, the preservation of the contract, the right to return to the same job and protection from detriment and dismissal match those for paternity leave.

Statutory paternity pay on adoption

The provisions for paternity pay on adoption are materially the same as those for statutory paternity pay.

Flexible working

Parents of children aged under 16, or of disabled children aged under 18, and carers of an adult living at the same address as the employee, or who is the spouse or partner of the employee or a relative of the employee, have the right to apply to work flexibly. Employers have a statutory duty to consider their applications seriously.

To be able to make a request for flexible working, the employee must:

- have worked for the employer continuously for at least 26 weeks on the date the application is made
- in the case of a parent, make the application no later than two weeks before the child's 16th birthday, or 18th birthday in the case of a disabled child
- have, or expect to have, responsibility for the child's upbringing or for providing care
- be making the application in order to care for the child or the other person for whom the employee is the carer
- not have made another application to work flexibly under this right in the past 12 months.

What changes can employees ask for?

They can request:

- a change in their hours of work
- a change to the times when they are required to work
- to work from home.

If a request is accepted, it will lead to a permanent change in the employee's terms and conditions of employment.

An employee who wishes to make an application to work flexibly must do so in writing. The application must state that it is a request for flexible working; the flexible working pattern that is applied for and the date on which the employee proposes it should start; how the employee meets the criteria for the relationship with the child or the other person for whom the employee is caring; and the effect of the change on the business and how this effect could be dealt with.

Within 28 days of the application being made, the employer must meet the employee to discuss it. The employee may, on request, be accompanied by a fellow employee at this meeting. If the proposed working pattern cannot be accommodated, other options can be considered.

Within 14 days of the meeting, the employer must write to the employee, either to agree on the new working pattern and a starting date for it, or to provide clear business grounds why the application cannot be accepted. The letter must set out the appeal procedure.

Appeal

The employer should hold a meeting to discuss any appeal by the employee within 14 days of receiving the submission of an appeal. The employee may, on request, be accompanied by a fellow employee at the appeal meeting.

The employee should notify the employee of its decision on the appeal within 14 days of the meeting. If the appeal is upheld, the employer's letter should state the contract variation that has been agreed on and the start date. If the employer dismisses the appeal, the letter should state the reasons for the decision and give sufficient explanation of why the decision was made.

These timescales can be extended by agreement between the employer and employee.

A meeting may be postponed for up to seven days if the employee's chosen work colleague is not available.

Can an employer refuse an application for flexible working?

It can only be refused for one, or more, of the following reasons:

- the burden of additional costs
- the detrimental effect on the ability to meet customers' demands
- the inability to reorganise work among the current staff
- the detrimental impact on quality or performance
- an inability to recruit
- insufficiency of work during the periods when the employee proposes to work
- planned structural changes.

Referral to the employment tribunal

An employee may refer a request if:

- the employer has not followed the procedure
- the decision was based on incorrect information
- the reason given for the refusal is not one that is specified.

The maximum compensation that the tribunal can award is 8 weeks' pay.

An employee has the right not to suffer a detriment, or to be dismissed, for seeking to exercise the right to request flexible working or for accompanying or seeking to accompany someone who wishes to exercise the right.

Parental leave

An employee with one year's service is entitled to take a total of 13 weeks' (or, for a disabled child, 18 weeks') unpaid parental leave for any purpose connected with the care of each child for whom the employee has parental responsibility. The right is to 13 (or 18) weeks' leave in total, with all employers.

The leave must be taken before:

- the child's fifth birthday, if the child is not disabled
- in the case of an adopted child who is not disabled, the fifth anniversary of the adoption, or the child's eighteenth birthday, whichever is earlier
- the child's eighteenth birthday, if the child is disabled.

Provisions of parental leave

Unless there is a separate collective agreement with a trade union or a workforce agreement with employees' representatives, the following provisions apply:

- the employee must have one year's service with the employer
- the employee must give the employer at least 21 days' notice of the intention to take parental leave and tell the employer the dates on which the leave is to start and finish
- the employee can take a maximum of four weeks' parental leave for any particular child in a particular year
- a period of leave that lasts less than a week counts as a week
- the employer has the right to postpone leave for up to six months on business grounds (except when leave is immediately after the birth of the child).

Referral to the employment tribunal

An employee who is refused the right to take parental leave, or whose employer postpones the leave unreasonably, may make a claim to the employment tribunal leading to an award of compensation.

An employee has the right not to suffer detrimental treatment by the employer for exercising the right to take parental leave.

Time off for dependants

A 'dependant' is a spouse, child, parent or person living in the employee's household as one of the family and, for the first three situations below, also a person for whom the employee is the primary carer.

An employee is entitled to reasonable unpaid time off work:

- to assist a dependant who is ill, injured or assaulted, or who gives birth
- to arrange care for an ill or injured dependant
- because of unexpected problems with a dependant's care arrangement
- in consequence of a dependant's death
- to deal with an unexpected incident, during school hours, affecting a child.

The right is only available if the employee tells the employer, as soon as possible, the reason for the absence and, if practicable, how long it is expected to last.

Referral to the employment tribunal

An employee who is refused time off may complain to the employment tribunal, with a possible award of compensation.

An employee has the right not to suffer detrimental treatment by the employer for exercising the right to take time off.

6. Trade union membership, duties and activities

6 Trade union membership, duties and activities

Time off

For officials

An official of a recognised independent union has the right to reasonable time off, with pay, for industrial relations duties and training. These must be concerned with matters under negotiation with the employer or with other functions that the employer has recognised as appropriate for the union.

For accredited learning representatives

Accredited learning representatives of a recognised independent union are entitled to reasonable time off with pay to carry out their duties (analysing training needs, advising members on learning, arranging training for members, consulting the employer and associated preparation) and to ensure that they are adequately trained for these functions.

For members

A member of a recognised independent union has the right to reasonable time off for union activities (not industrial action). There is no statutory right to pay for this time off.

Advisory, Conciliation and Arbitration Service (ACAS) Code of Practice 'Time Off for Trade Union Duties and Activities' clarifies these rights. 'Duties' are defined and those items listed as 'activities' cannot be claimed as union duties that attract a mandatory payment.

Inducements

A worker has the right not to be induced by the employer:

- not to be a member of an independent trade union
- not to take part in the activities of an independent trade union
- not to make use of a trade union's services
- to be a member of a trade union or

- if he or she is a member of a recognised union (or one seeking recognition), to adopt terms of employment that will not be determined by a collective agreement negotiated by that union.

An employee (or worker) can complain to the employment tribunal that the employer has attempted such inducement. A successful complaint attracts an award of £3,100.

Victimisation

A worker has the general right to apply to the employment tribunal claiming that an employer has taken action short of dismissal (such as withholding opportunities for transfer, training and promotion) against her or him as an individual:

- to prevent, deter or penalise the worker for membership of an independent trade union
- to prevent, deter or penalise the worker for participation in the activities of an independent trade union or for making use of its services
- to compel the worker to join a union
- to penalise the worker for involvement in union recognition or de-recognition
- because of the worker's failure to accept an inducement.

The remedy is a complaint to the employment tribunal for a declaration and compensation (an amount that the tribunal considers just and equitable reparation for the loss).

The employer and/or worker can join a third party (person or trade union) who, they claim, induced the alleged victimisation by actual or threatened industrial action. The tribunal may order the person or trade union to pay part or all of any award.

Legislation is scheduled for introduction in 2010 to regulate the use of 'blacklists' of trade union members or activists. Employment tribunals will be able to hear claims by individuals that they were refused or dismissed from employment or treated detrimentally in employment for being on a prohibited blacklist. The courts will also have powers to award damages or issue injunctions relating to the use of blacklists.

7. Miscellaneous statutory rights

7 Miscellaneous statutory rights

Health and safety

Time off

Safety representatives nominated by trade unions or elected by employees are entitled to reasonable paid time off to perform functions and undergo appropriate training.

Victimisation

An employee has the right to complain to an employment tribunal of detrimental treatment by the employer arising from the following actions by the employee:

- undertaking activities in connection with reducing risks to health and safety (having been designated by the employer to undertake such activities)
- performing functions as an acknowledged safety representative or member of a safety committee
- taking part in consultation with the employer on safety matters or in an election of employee representatives in accordance with specific regulations
- bringing to the employer's attention, by reasonable means, matters believed to be harmful to health and safety (if either there is no safety representative or committee, or it is not practicable to contact them)
- leaving or refusing to return to a place of work in circumstances of serious and imminent danger
- taking steps to protect himself or herself or others from serious and imminent danger.

In most of the above, proposed action by the employee of the type described is also protected.

The remedy is a complaint to the employment tribunal for a declaration and compensation (an amount that the tribunal considers just and equitable reparation for the loss).

Employees' representatives

Time off

An employee who is an employees' representative for the purposes of consultation (see Chapter 12) or a candidate for such a post has the right to reasonable time off with pay to undertake relevant functions.

Enforcement is by a claim to the employment tribunal, which will award a successful claimant the amount of pay for the time off denied or not paid for.

Victimisation

The employee has the right not to be subjected to any detrimental treatment by his or her employer on the grounds that, as an employees' representative or as a candidate in an election for that post, he or she performed, or proposed to perform, relevant functions or activities.

Enforcement is by a claim to the employment tribunal, which may award compensation having regard to the nature of the breach and the employee's resultant loss.

Trustees of occupational pension schemes

Time off

An employee who is a trustee of an occupational pension scheme has the right to reasonable time off with pay to perform appropriate duties or undergo relevant training.

Victimisation

An employee has the right not to be subjected to any detrimental treatment on the grounds that he or she performed or proposed to perform any relevant functions as a trustee of an occupational pension scheme in that employment.

Sunday working

'Protected' and opted-out shop workers and betting workers have the right not to be subjected to any detrimental treatment for refusing to work on Sundays. All shop workers and betting workers have the right not to be treated detrimentally for opting out or proposing to do so. The remedy is a complaint to the employment tribunal for a declaration and compensation.

Time off for public duties

The right is to reasonable time off to undertake public duties. There is no statutory right to pay for this time off. Public duties include duties as:

- a Justice of the Peace
- a member of a local authority
- a statutory tribunal
- a police authority
- an independent monitoring board for a prison or prison visiting committee
- a relevant health or education body
- the Environment Agency
- Scottish Water or a Water Customer Consultation Panel.

'Reasonable' time off depends on the circumstances.

Jury service

An employee has the right not to be subjected to any detrimental treatment on the grounds that he or she has been summoned to attend jury service or is or has been absent from work for that purpose.

However, the employer's failure to pay the employee for such absence will not be detrimental treatment if the contract does not provide for payment.

Time off when under notice of redundancy

A redundant employee with two years' continuous service is entitled to reasonable time off during the notice period to look for work or arrange for training. The employer must pay the employee, at the appropriate rate, to a maximum of two-fifths of a week's pay.

The employment tribunal can award two-fifths of a week's pay if it finds an employer has unreasonably refused the employee time off.

Requests for time to train

From April 2010 for employers with at least 250 employees and from April 2011 for other employers, employees' with twenty-six weeks' service will have the right to request time off from normal duties to undertake training that will enhance their knowledge and skills and the performance of the business.

The employer will be under a duty to consider the request according to a procedure that is very similar to that used for requests for flexible working (see Chapter 5). The request may be denied if there are good business reasons for doing so or if the employer believes that the training will not enhance the business.

Disclosure in the public interest

An employee may apply to the employment tribunal for compensation if subjected to a detriment by the employer as a result of making a 'protected disclosure' of information about an alleged wrongdoing ('whistleblowing').

Under the Public Interest Disclosure Act, the information being disclosed must relate to one of the following:

- a criminal offence
- a failure to comply with a legal obligation
- a miscarriage of justice
- endangering the health and safety of an individual
- damage to the environment
- concealment of any of the above.

To qualify for protection, the employee must follow the methods of disclosure specified by the Act. The disclosure must:

- be made in 'good faith'
- normally be made to the employee's employer or a legal adviser. If a worker's employer is an individual appointed by a Minister of the Crown, disclosure must be to a Minister of the Crown.

A grievance about the employer's alleged failure to comply with contractual (legal) obligations to the employee is capable of being treated as a 'protected disclosure' by the employee.

Data protection

In general terms, data should be processed in accordance with the Data Protection Act. The Employment Practices Data Protection Code – 2005 provides guidance.

Most employers process data, which means that they must be registered with the Information Commissioner as doing so. A failure to register gives rise to a criminal offence. Records held manually and by computer are both covered by the Act.

Employees' access to their personal data

Employees are entitled to see what data are held on them, provided that their requests are made in writing. Access to the data must normally be given within 40 days of the request. If the data identify a third person, the employee does not have an automatic right to see those data. Either the consent of the third party must first be obtained, or identifying features must be removed.

References

There is no general legal duty to provide a reference about an employee or ex-employee. Employers should, however, be mindful of any potential claim for victimisation, during employment or post-employment, under the various anti-discrimination laws.

When a reference is provided, there is a legal duty of care, both to the person it is about and to the person it is being sent to. This requirement can be met if the reference is factual and fair.

Accompaniment at disciplinary and grievance hearings

A worker has the right, on request, to be accompanied at any grievance or disciplinary hearing by a work colleague or trade union representative.

A grievance hearing is a meeting to discuss a failure by an employer to perform a duty in relation to a worker.

A disciplinary hearing is one which could result in a formal warning, some other action or the confirmation of a warning or other action (that is, an appeal).

The hearing should be rescheduled (maximum five-day postponement) if the chosen companion cannot attend.

What the companion is allowed to do

The companion (who must be allowed paid time off work) is permitted:

- to put the worker's case
- to sum up that case
- to respond on the worker's behalf to any view expressed at the hearing but not to answer questions on behalf of the worker.

What if the employer refuses to allow the worker to be accompanied?

The remedy is a complaint to the employment tribunal and an award of up to two weeks' pay. A worker may seek compensation from the employment tribunal if subjected to a detriment for exercising the right to be accompanied or for acting as the companion of another worker.

The ACAS statutory Code of Practice on disciplinary and grievance procedures

This provides practical guidance and sets out the principles for handling disciplinary and grievance matters. The employment tribunal will take the code into account when considering relevant cases. It can adjust any award by up to 25% for unreasonable failure to comply with the code. So, if the tribunal feels that an employer has unreasonably failed to follow the guidance in the code, it can increase an award. If it feels an employee has failed to follow the guidance, it can reduce any award by up to 25%.

Medical reports

For employment or insurance reasons an employer may obtain a report from a medical practitioner who is responsible for the clinical care of an employee. Before the employer can get the report, the employee must be told that the employer is to apply for the medical information and the employee must give consent.

The employee must also be told his or her rights in relation to the report. These are:

- to withhold consent to the application for the report or the disclosure of its contents
- to see the report before it is given to the employer
- to ask for a copy of the report within six months of its supply
- to amend any part of the report that he or she considers inaccurate or misleading.

A medical practitioner may refuse to allow a person to see a report if doing so would cause serious physical or mental harm, or would reveal the identity of someone who has supplied information for the report.

8. Diversity and non-discrimination

8 Diversity and non-discrimination

Laws promoting diversity

It is generally unlawful to treat a person less favourably (discriminate against him or her) in a number of specified situations because of sex, sexual orientation, race, religion or belief, disability and age. For most purposes, the intention of the alleged discriminator is irrelevant to whether or not discrimination has occurred and whether it is unlawful.

This principle applies to the treatment of people in relation to employment, training (including training under government schemes), and contract work. So, the protections and rights extend to those who are not employees but who are contracted to provide services personally.

General discrimination

Less favourable treatment (general discrimination) is unlawful if it manifests itself in:

- differential selection arrangements
- a refusal or deliberate omission to offer employment
- offering different terms of employment
- differential terms in employment
- differential access to opportunities for promotion, transfer or training; or to benefits, facilities or services or
- dismissal or other detriment.

There are also two, specifically-defined forms of unlawful discrimination – victimisation and harassment.

Acts of discrimination that occur after employment has ended are unlawful if they arise out of and are closely connected to the previous employment relationship.

It is also generally unlawful:

- to publish a job advertisement that might reasonably be understood to indicate an intention to discriminate

- to instruct, induce or attempt to induce another person to discriminate unlawfully.

A person who, in the course of employment, aids another to do an unlawful act is treated as doing that act.

Application to the employment tribunal

Enforcement by individuals is by application to the employment tribunal within three months of the act complained of, but a tribunal may admit an 'out of time' case, if it considers it 'just and equitable' to do so. ACAS conciliation is always available. The tribunal has three possible remedies:

- a declaration: a statement of the rights of the claimant and in what respect the employer or any employee has acted unlawfully
- compensation: an **uncapped amount** for injury to feelings and any financial losses
- recommendations: to benefit the employee and lessen the effect of the discrimination.

Injured feelings

An employment tribunal can award compensation for 'injury to feelings' in discrimination cases. The so-called 'Vento guidelines' were first established in 2002 and have since been updated to take account of inflation. There are three bands:

- £18,000–£30,000 for the most serious cases, such as where there has been a lengthy campaign of harassment. An award over £30,000 would be exceptional
- £6,000–£18,000 for serious cases that do not merit the highest band
- £500–£6,000 for less serious cases, such as an isolated act of discrimination. The guidelines say awards of less than £500 should be avoided.

In determining fair and reasonable compensation, tribunals are advised to have regard to the 'overall magnitude of the sum total of compensation for non-pecuniary loss made under the various headings of injury to feelings, psychiatric damage and aggravated damage'.

Liability

Managers and others can be personally liable. An organisation will be liable for discrimination by its employees, unless it successfully relies on the defence of having taken reasonably practicable steps to prevent the unlawful act (for example, by issuing policies on, or providing training in, diversity).

The Equality and Human Rights Commission

This body performs other enforcement and education functions. Its powers include investigation, obtaining information, issuing non-discrimination notices, applying for an injunction against persistent offenders and applying for a declaration of rights.

Sex discrimination

The legislation covers:

- sex discrimination (for either sex)
- discrimination against married people and
- discrimination against people who intend to undergo, are undergoing or have undergone, gender reassignment.

There are four major forms of discrimination:

Direct –
treating a person, by act or omission, less favourably than another on the grounds of that person's sex; or treating a married person less favourably than an unmarried person of the same sex on the grounds of marital status; or on the grounds of gender reassignment, treating a person less favourably than another who has not undergone gender reassignment.

Harassment –
subjecting a person to unwanted conduct related to a person's sex (whether the sex of that person or of another person), or subjecting a person to unwanted conduct on the ground of gender reassignment, either of which has the purpose or effect of violating the person's dignity or creating an intimidating, hostile, degrading, humiliating or offensive environment.

An employer can also be directly liable for failing to take reasonable steps to prevent an employee being subjected to sex-related harassment by one or more third parties (anybody not employed by the employer) when the employer is aware that the employee has been subject to third-party harassment on at least two previous occasions.

Indirect –
applying to all people a provision, criterion or practice that puts, or would put, one sex, or married people, at a particular disadvantage and which cannot be shown to be 'a proportionate means of achieving a legitimate aim' (that is, objectively justified).

Victimisation –
taking action against anyone for asserting rights under the Sex Discrimination Act or the Equal Pay Act or for giving evidence or information in proceedings in this connection.

The exceptions are –
discrimination in the provisions made for death or retirement is not unlawful. But the compulsory retirement of a woman earlier than a man is unlawful discrimination and unfair dismissal.

Discrimination that is necessary to comply with statutory provisions to protect women against risks specific to them, such as pregnancy and maternity.

If gender is a 'genuine occupational qualification' for a job.

Code of practice

This is issued by the former Equal Opportunities Commission and provides guidance on avoiding sex discrimination (including the establishment of an equal opportunities policy).

Potential discrimination in promotion

The Sex Discrimination Act provides that it is unlawful to discriminate against an employee 'in the way he affords her access to opportunities for promotion..'. The possibility of discrimination in internal promotion is much greater if there is no formal selection procedure in place, and promotion is based on managerial discretion.

If promotion is refused because the employer believes a woman would not 'fit in' with the male-dominated culture of existing senior managers, then a tribunal may infer that discrimination has tainted the promotion process.

A woman absent on maternity leave who is not informed of possible promotion opportunities also has a potential claim. In VISA International Service Association v Paul, the Employment Appeal Tribunal said that a failure to alert a pregnant woman on maternity leave to a job for which she would have been likely to consider herself suitable subjected her to a detriment because of her pregnancy. It was a breach of the implied term of trust and confidence entitling her to resign and claim constructive dismissal.

Equal pay (sex discrimination)

Equality is required in terms and conditions of employment (including rates of pay and pensions) for men and women. Contracts of employment are deemed to contain an 'equality clause' and occupational pension schemes an 'equal treatment rule'. Each secures equal pay/pensions if a female and a male are both employed:

- 'in the same employment', that is, in the same 'establishment', or in another establishment of the same, or an associated employer, where common terms and conditions are applied either generally or to relevant employees, and are also employed...
- 'on like work', which is work of the same or a broadly similar nature and the differences in frequency, nature and extent are not of practical importance, or...

- 'on work rated as equivalent' by a job evaluation study under various headings of demands made. If the method of job evaluation has treated men and women differently under any heading and but for this a woman's job would have been given equal value, the work may be rated as equivalent or...
- 'on work of equal value', where the demands made on an employee under, for instance, such headings as effort, skill and decision-making are determined by a tribunal to be of equal value to those made upon an employee of the opposite sex, even though the work is not 'like work'.

Possible defence

The employer will have a defence if it can demonstrate that the variation in pay (which includes terms of employment other than pay) is due to a 'material difference' between either employees or their jobs that is not a difference based on gender. In claims of 'equal value', this is extended to any material factor (other than gender) justifying the differences in pay.

Enforcement by the employment tribunal

Enforcement and remedy are through application to the employment tribunal for a declaration of rights and (except in cases of equal treatment regarding pensions) for arrears of remuneration or for damages normally covering six years (or, in Scotland, five years). For pensions, the employer is under a duty to provide the pension scheme with the necessary funds to ensure equality.

A claim for equal pay to the employment tribunal must normally be made within six months of the employment ending.

Collective agreements

Terms of collective agreements that are discriminatory are void.

Exceptions are provisions relating to retirement or death and the rights under the law relating to special treatment accorded to women in connection with pregnancy or childbirth.

Sexual orientation discrimination

The legislation applies to heterosexual, homosexual and bisexual people of either sex.

There are four major forms of discrimination:

Direct –
treating one person less favourably than another on the grounds of that person's sexual orientation.

Harassment –
on grounds of sexual orientation, subjecting a person to unwanted conduct which has the purpose or effect of violating the person's dignity or creating an intimidating, hostile, degrading, humiliating or offensive environment.

Indirect –
applying to all people a provision, criterion or practice which puts or would put people of a particular sexual orientation at a particular disadvantage and which cannot be shown to be a 'proportionate means of achieving a legitimate aim' (that is, objectively justified).

Victimisation –
taking action against anyone for asserting rights under the legislation or for giving evidence or information in proceedings in that connection.

and an exception –
it is not unlawful to discriminate if sexual orientation is a 'genuine and determining occupational requirement' for a job and it is proportionate to apply that requirement.

Racial discrimination

Legislation makes discrimination on grounds of race unlawful. Discrimination occurs if there is less favourable treatment 'on racial grounds' or of a 'racial group'. Both expressions are defined by reference to colour, race, nationality, or ethnic or national origins.

There are four major forms of discrimination

Direct –
treating one person less favourably than another on the grounds of that person's race.

Harassment –
on grounds of race, subjecting a person to unwanted conduct which has the purpose or effect of violating the person's dignity or creating an intimidating, hostile, degrading, humiliating or offensive environment.

Indirect –
applying to all people a provision, criterion or practice which puts or would put people of a particular race at a particular disadvantage and which cannot be shown to be a 'proportionate means of achieving a legitimate aim' (that is, objectively justified).

Victimisation –
taking action against anyone for asserting rights under the legislation or for giving evidence or information in proceedings in that connection.

The legislation does not apply:

- to work that is not done at an establishment in Great Britain
- to training to meet the needs of a racial group under-represented in a particular occupation
- if race is a 'genuine occupational qualification'.

Code of practice

This is issued by the former Commission for Racial Equality and provides guidance on avoiding racial discrimination (including the establishment of an equal opportunities policy).

Religious or belief-based discrimination

Legislation covers discrimination on the grounds of religion, belief or a lack of religion or belief. Religion or belief is defined as any religion, religious belief or philosophical belief.

There are four major forms of discrimination

Direct –
treating one person less favourably than another on the grounds of that person's religion or belief. Direct discrimination extends to 'associative' discrimination (that is, discrimination motivated by the characteristics of a person with whom the victim of discrimination associates or is associated).

Harassment –
on grounds of religion or belief, subjecting a person to unwanted conduct which has the purpose or effect of violating the person's dignity or creating an intimidating, hostile, degrading, humiliating or offensive environment.

Indirect –
applying to all people a provision, criterion or practice which puts or would put people of a particular religion or belief at a particular disadvantage and which cannot be shown to be a 'proportionate means of achieving a legitimate aim' (that is, objectively justified).

Victimisation –
taking action against anyone for asserting rights under the legislation or for giving evidence or information in proceedings in that connection.

and an exception –
it is not unlawful to discriminate if religion or belief is a 'genuine and determining occupational requirement' for a job and it is proportionate to apply that requirement.

Your belief / my belief

A belief that mankind is heading towards catastrophic climate change and that people should live their lives in a way that would reduce or avoid that catastrophe can amount to a philosophical belief and fall within the legislation that outlaws discrimination on grounds of religion or belief.

The Employment Equality (Religion or Belief) Regulations prevent discrimination, victimisation or harassment on the ground of religion or belief. The Employment Appeal Tribunal (Grainger plc and others v Nicholson) found that a claimant's belief in climate change fell within the limits of what might constitute a philosophical belief.

The EAT said that a 'belief' must be:

- genuinely held
- a belief, not an opinion or viewpoint
- a belief about a weighty and substantial aspect of human life and behaviour
- able to attain a certain level of cogency, seriousness, cohesion and importance
- worthy of respect in a democratic society, not incompatible with human dignity and not in conflict with the fundamental rights of others.

Disability discrimination

Legislation protects disabled people from discrimination. A disabled person is someone with a physical or mental impairment that has a substantial and long-term adverse effect on the ability to carry out normal day-to-day activities.

People who become disabled, or whose condition worsens, during employment are covered by the Disability Discrimination Act.

Discrimination may occur in five ways

Harassment –
subjecting a person to unwanted conduct related to a person's disability (whether the disability of that person or the disability of another person,

which has the purpose or effect of violating the person's dignity or creating an intimidating, hostile, degrading, humiliating or offensive environment.

An employer can also be directly liable for failing to take reasonable steps to prevent an employee being subjected to disability-related harassment by one or more third parties (anybody not employed by the employer) when the employer is aware that the employee has been subject to third-party harassment on at least two previous occasions.

Victimisation –
taking action against anyone for asserting rights under the Disability Discrimination Act or for giving evidence or information in proceedings in this connection.

'Disability-related' –
the employer, for a reason related to a person's disability, treats that person less favourably than other people are treated, or would be treated, and the employer cannot show justification for the treatment.

Less favourable treatment of a disabled person is justified only if the reason for it relates to the individual circumstances and is not trivial or minor. Less favourable treatment is justified if a person cannot do the job or if there is no practicable adjustment (see below) that would enable the person to do it.

'Direct' –
the employer treats a disabled person less favourably than a person who does not have that disability but whose relevant circumstances are not materially different from those of the disabled person.

and/or

'Adjustments' –
the employer does not comply with the duty imposed by the Disability Discrimination Act to make reasonable adjustments if the employment arrangements or premises place disabled people at a substantial disadvantage.

The duty to make reasonable adjustments includes:

- the approach to, exit from, or access to buildings
- the fixtures, fittings, furniture and equipment
- the arrangements for deciding to whom employment is offered
- the terms or conditions relating to employment, promotion, transfer and training either before or during employment.

Factors determining whether an employer should make adjustments are the effectiveness, practicability and cost to the employer of the change.

Compliance with the duty to make reasonable adjustments may entail giving a suitably-qualified disabled person priority over a better-qualified non-disabled person (in essence, a form of 'positive discrimination').

Exclusions

Provisions related to certain pension scheme benefits and performance-related pay can lawfully discriminate against disabled persons.

Code of practice

Guidance for the elimination of discrimination in employment is issued by the Secretary of State.

Age discrimination

Legislation makes discrimination on grounds of age ('young' or 'old') unlawful.

There are four major forms of discrimination

Direct –
treating one person less favourably than another on the grounds of age, if that treatment is not a proportionate means of achieving a legitimate aim (that is, the treatment can be objectively justified).

Harassment –
on the grounds of age, subjecting a person to unwanted conduct which has the purpose or effect of violating the person's dignity or creating an intimidating, hostile, degrading, humiliating or offensive environment.

Indirect –
applying a provision, criterion or practice to a person of a particular 'age group' that puts people in that age group, at a particular disadvantage compared with other people and which is not 'a proportionate means of achieving a legitimate aim'.

Victimisation –
taking action against someone for asserting rights under the relevant legislation or for giving evidence or information in proceedings in that connection.

Exceptions

- if having a characteristic related to age is a 'genuine and determining occupational requirement' for a job and it is proportionate to apply that requirement
- the quantification of benefits (for example, paid holidays) by reference to a period of service of up to 5 years. Thereafter, any continuing lower level of benefit must be justified as fulfilling a 'business need'
- the provision of enhanced redundancy payments, provided that the employer uses the statutory redundancy payment tariff as the initial basis of calculation
- not offering employment to someone who is, or within 6 months will be, at or beyond an employer's 'normal retirement age' of 65 or over, or, if there is no such normal retirement age, aged 65
- subject to the satisfaction of certain criteria, dismissing an employee at or over the age of 65 for reason of 'retirement'.

Procedure for potentially lawful 'compulsory' retirement (only at or over age 65)

At least 6 months, but no more than 12 months, before the intended retirement date, an employer must notify an employee, in writing, of that date. The notification should also tell the employee of the right to request not to retire. Failure to comply with this duty to notify may result in an award of compensation of up to 8 weeks' pay.

Whether or not an employer has served the notification, an employee may make a written request not to retire and, if the employee does so, must say whether he or she wishes to continue indefinitely or until a specified date.

The request must be submitted between 3 and 6 months before the intended retirement date or, if no notification has been given by employer, at any time in the 6 months before that date.

An employer must hold a meeting with the employee to discuss the request, within a reasonable period of receiving it, unless:

- the parties agree during that period that the employee will retire later; or
- it is not reasonably practicable to do so (then, the employer must still consider the request).

Following the meeting or consideration of the request, the employer must give the employee written confirmation of its decision and, if that is:

- to have the employee retire on the intended retirement date; or
- to keep the employee on, but for a shorter time than the employee requested, then

the employer must inform the employee of the right of appeal. The appeal process is the same as for the original consideration of the request.

The employee is entitled, on request, to be accompanied by a colleague (not a trade union official) at the original and appeal meetings. An employer's failure to allow accompaniment may result in award of compensation of up to 2 weeks' pay.

The procedure has important implications for fairness of a 'retirement' dismissal (see Chapter 10).

Discrimination against part-time workers

A part-time worker is one with hours of work that are less than those of a full-time worker employed by the same employer, doing the same work and having the same type of contract. (So, strictly, someone who works 35 hours a week rather than the full 37.5 normally required would be a part-timer.)

Part-time workers have the right not to be treated less favourably than such a 'comparable' full-time worker, unless the employer can justify that treatment. This covers terms and conditions of employment (usually 'pro rata' equality is required) or any other detriment.

Employees have the right to request from the employer a written explanation if they believe they are being treated less favourably than a comparable full-time employee. The employer must respond within 21 days. Deliberate and unreasonable failure to reply, or evasive or equivocal answers, can lead to the inference of discrimination.

The remedy is a complaint of discrimination to the employment tribunal, which may make a declaration and/or an award of compensation. There is also protection against victimisation for relying on these rights.

Discrimination against fixed-term employees

A 'fixed-term contract' is one that terminates on the expiry of a period of time, the completion of a particular task or the occurrence or non-occurrence of a specified event. A contract with one of these features remains a 'fixed-term contract' even if it contains a provision for earlier termination by the giving of notice. The Employment Rights Act refers to the same range of contracts as 'limited-term contracts'.

Employees on fixed-term contracts ('fixed-term employees') should not be treated less favourably than comparable, 'permanent' employees on the grounds that they are fixed-term employees, unless this is objectively justified.

Treatment of fixed-term employees

Fixed-term employees can compare themselves to employees of the same employer who are not on fixed-term contracts and who do the same or broadly similar work. If there is no comparable 'permanent' employee in the establishment, a comparison can be made with a similar permanent employee working for the employer in a different establishment.

Treatment may be assessed in two ways:

- by reference to any one of the fixed-term employee's terms and conditions of employment, which should be not less favourable than the comparable 'permanent' employee's, or
- by reference to the fixed-term employee's overall package of terms and conditions of employment, which should not be less favourable.

What if fixed-term employees feel they are being treated unfairly?

Employees have the right to request from the employer a written explanation if they believe they are being treated less favourably than a comparable 'permanent' employee. The employer must respond within 21 days. Deliberate and unreasonable failure to reply, or evasive or equivocal answers, can lead to the inference of discrimination.

Limitation on successive contracts

The use of successive fixed-term contracts is limited to four years' service, unless the use of further fixed-term contracts is justified on objective grounds. So, if there is no such justification, a fixed-term contract renewed after the four-year period of service will be treated as a contract for an indefinite period.

Waiver clauses

Any clause that still exists in a fixed-term contract that purports to deny the right to claim unfair dismissal and/or to claim a statutory redundancy payment on the expiry of that contract without renewal (a dismissal - see chapter 10) is now invalid.

Access to permanent work

Fixed-term employees should be given information on permanent vacancies in the organisation.

Referral to the employment tribunal

The remedy is a complaint of discrimination to the employment tribunal for a declaration and/or compensation. There is also protection against victimisation for relying on rights.

Discrimination against convicted offenders

After a period of good behaviour, a conviction is 'spent' – that is, treated as if it had never occurred. Rehabilitation periods for those aged 18 or over when found guilty include:

- Prison or young offenders' institution (YOI) sentence of between 6 months and 2½ years — 10 years
- Prison or YOI sentence of 6 months or less — 7 years
- Fine, probation order or community service order — 5 years
- Conditional discharge — 1 year or order or binding over period if longer
- Absolute discharge — 6 months.

Job applicants cannot be required to disclose spent convictions. These should not be used as grounds for discrimination in recruitment, during employment or as reason for dismissal.

However, there is no specific protection or remedy for breach of this principle, except when someone with at least one year's service is dismissed and can claim unfair dismissal (see Chapter 10). Otherwise, the only possible redress is action for defamation, a declaration or an injunction.

Exceptions

Among the jobs that the right of non-disclosure of spent convictions does not apply to are medical practitioners, vets, nurses, lawyers, accountants, police, traffic wardens, teachers, social workers and youth workers. It does, however, apply to security workers.

9. Changes to the employment relationship

9 Changes to the employment relationship

Changing the identity of the employer – Transfer of Undertakings

Under the Transfer of Undertakings (Protection of Employment) Regulations 2006, known as TUPE, employees' rights are safeguarded when there is a 'relevant transfer' of a business or undertaking, or part of it, to a new employer. A 'relevant transfer' is either:

- the transfer (by sale or otherwise) of all or part of a business or undertaking if that 'economic entity retains its identity' and/or
- a 'service provision change' (covering contracting-out, change of contractors following re-tendering, and contracting-in).

Transfers by acquisition of shares are excluded, because there is no change in the legal personality of the organisation employing people.

But the passing of an 'economic entity' (for example, a division or department) between two subsidiaries in the same 'group' will generally come within TUPE.

Automatic continuation of employment contracts

An employee can exercise the right to object to being transferred, in which case the contract of employment comes to an end. If there is no objection, then the contract of employment of someone employed at the time of a transfer does not terminate. It automatically continues as if it had been made with the new employer ('transferee'). The new employer takes over the liabilities of the old employer ('transferor'), with the exception of criminal liabilities.

This effect is excluded, along with the specific provisions on dismissal, if the transferor is the subject of bankruptcy or similar insolvency proceedings that have commenced with a view to the liquidation of assets (therefore, not all insolvency situations).

The 'automatic continuation' effect applies to an employee dismissed before the transfer but for a transfer-related reason that is unfair. In that case the liability for the unfair dismissal passes to the new employer.

Employee liability information for the new employer

Before a transfer, the transferor and transferee must each inform (and if measures are envisaged in relation to their own employees, consult with) representatives of its own employees affected by the forthcoming transfer.

The transferor must supply the transferee with 'employee liability information' in writing at least 14 days before the transfer or, otherwise, as soon as reasonably practicable.

The employee liability information must cover:

- the identity and age of transferring employees
- information covered by their statements of employment particulars
- details of any applicable collective agreements
- disciplinary and grievance cases in the preceding two years
- legal actions in the preceding two years and ones that are reasonably expected.

The information must be accurate to a specified date no more than 14 days before it is communicated. Subsequent changes must be notified by the transferor. The information may be provided in instalments and/or through a third party.

What if employee liability information is not supplied?

A transferee's remedy for the transferor's failure to provide the information is a complaint to the employment tribunal, which can award compensation (normally a minimum of £500 per employee in respect of whom there was non-compliance).

Objecting to a transfer

In a TUPE situation, if an employee objects to transferring to the new employer, the contract of employment does not transfer and the effect is to terminate the contract with the original employer. The termination of employment will not normally amount to a dismissal.

Pension scheme arrangements

Transferring employees who were offered an occupational pension scheme by the old employer must be offered any one of the following types of scheme by the new employer:

- defined benefit (if the transferee chooses this option, the scheme must comply with minimum standards)
- defined contribution ('money purchase') or
- stakeholder.

Transferee employers choosing to offer a defined contribution or stakeholder scheme must match the employees' contributions to a maximum of 6% of earnings.

Changes to terms and conditions of transferred employees

Changes made for a transfer-related reason are void unless they are a) by agreement and b) for an 'economic, technical or organisational reason entailing changes in the workforce'.

Less stringent requirements apply on changing terms for insolvent businesses if the changes have the purpose of ensuring survival and safeguarding employment opportunities.

Changing terms on transfer

A change in a contractual term that is 'transfer-related' is likely to be void. This can also apply to the introduction of restrictive covenants following a transfer. In one case (Credit Suisse First Boston(Europe) Limited v Lister), after a TUPE transfer, as part of a deal to retain the employee, the new employer inserted a non-compete clause into the contract. The employee challenged the clause and it was held to be 'transfer-related' and so void, even though the employer had given the employee a 'consideration' of £65,000.

Avoiding a two-tier workforce

An employer taking over a service that was provided by a local authority or other public sector organisation should be aware of the government's codes of practice on the avoidance of a two-tier workforce (that is, people working alongside one another on different terms and conditions of service).

Changing the content of the contract: terms and conditions

How a change can be made

Broadly, there are three possible approaches.

1 Mutual agreement between employer and employee:
- on an ad hoc basis, when the need arises; or
- through a 'standing' clause in the contract, allowing a party to amend content.

This is based on the premise that, just as the contract is established by agreement, so it can be varied in the same way (subject to limitation under TUPE – Transfer of Undertakings – see above) without there being a breach of contract.

2 Unilateral implementation:
- under contractual authority (effectively, the same as above – therefore, there would be no breach of contract); or
- without contractual authority – a clear breach of contract.

3 Termination of the current contract with due notice and the offer of its immediate replacement with a new contract containing the revised term(s). Here, because the first contract is brought to an end in accordance with its own terms (the notice clause), there will be no breach of contract.

Other legal requirements

If the change involves both a breach of contract and the loss of a financial amount (for example, a reduction in pay), the employee will have the right to sue for any lost amount(s) falling due for payment while the contract continues in being. The employee's action might be either for damages in the County or High Courts or for one or more unlawful deductions from 'wages' in the employment tribunal.

A breach of contract will, if sufficiently serious, also entitle the employee to resign and to treat him- or herself as 'constructively' dismissed.

Dismissals resulting from a change – possible defence

Any dismissal involved in the change, whether 'constructive' or by termination effected directly by the employer, may be fair if the reason for the change is sufficiently important for the business ('some other substantial reason') and there has been prior consultation with the employee in an attempt to obtain agreement to the change. However, in the absence of either of these elements, it will be unfair and will allow the employee to receive compensation for financial loss, even if the employee accepted an offer of continued employment under a new contract.

Changes that might affect 20 or more employees

If the change is intended to affect 20 or more employees at a single establishment, there will also be the requirement for the employer to consult with employees' representatives about proposed dismissals for redundancy. The definitions of 'redundancy' and 'proposed dismissal' under this law are sufficiently wide to include almost any wide-scale change to contracts of employment.

10. Terminating the contract

10 Terminating the contract

Notice

The statutory minimum notice due, on dismissal, to an employee with at least one month's continuous service is:

- one week's notice if he or she has been employed for less than two years
- one week's notice for each year of continuous employment between two years and eleven years and
- twelve weeks' notice for twelve or more years' continuous employment.

The statutory minimum notice due from an employee (on resignation) is one week.

If the contractual notice is greater than the applicable statutory minimum, the contractual notice prevails.

A common misconception (2)

'...an employee's notice of resignation can be refused'

It cannot, just as an employee cannot reject the employer's notice of dismissal. Of course, you can try to persuade employees to stay. Alternatively, you can relieve them of the obligation to work out their notice and pay them off. Or, if your concern is about their joining a competitor, you can rely on any enforceable contractual provisions restraining post-termination activity or about 'garden leave'.

If an employee gives notice of resignation while facing a charge of serious misconduct, an employer is fully entitled to continue with the disciplinary process during the notice period – only a resignation with instant effect can stop that.

If notice is worked, the employee is entitled to all contractual payments and benefits. And if the contractual notice required from the employer does not exceed the applicable statutory minimum by more than six days, the employee has the statutory right to full pay for any day in the notice period when he or she is absent through sickness, pregnancy, maternity/paternity/adoption leave or a lack of work and would not otherwise be entitled to full pay (for example, in relation to sickness, when the employee's entitlement to sick pay has expired).

Exactly when is 'notice' of termination given?

Regardless of the required contractual or statutory length, 'notice' is a very particular, if often basic, thing. It contains a specific date, or the information necessary to calculate the specific date, on which the contract of employment will terminate.

A mere intimation of possible dismissal or confirmation of a decision to dismiss at some time in the future (even if the likely period during which the dismissal will occur is stated) will not amount to proper 'notice'. This has implications for an employer's liability to provide pay in lieu of notice when the contract is later terminated.

Common misconception (3)

'...notice given can be cancelled'

The cancellation of notice is only legally possible if the party to whom the notice was given agrees to it being annulled. Otherwise, the notice stands and the termination will take effect.

Of course, there may be various practical or economic considerations that persuade the party receiving notice to agree quite readily to its cancellation. And there may be disadvantages imposed by legislation on someone who declines to stay in employment (for example, see the provisions on redundancy payments and suitable alternative employment in Chapter 11). But the contractual principle remains – agreement is the key.

Wrongful dismissal

Wrongful dismissal is a dismissal that is in breach of contract.

Dismissal without any notice (summary dismissal) or without full notice is wrongful, unless the employee's conduct amounts to repudiation (for example, gross misconduct/negligence), or if the contract permits it (through a pay in lieu of notice, PILON, clause) as an alternative to working notice.

If the dismissal is wrongful, the employer can pay in lieu of all or part of the employee's notice entitlement (in effect, damages for breach of contract), but:

- the employer will be unable to enforce provisions restraining the ex-employee's post-termination activity; and
- the dismissal can still be unfair.

The employee's remedy for wrongful dismissal is an action to recover financial loss (through an award of damages), either in the employment tribunal (maximum award £25,000) or civil court (no limit).

A dismissal with notice is not normally a breach of contract (but the dismissal can still be unfair under legislation).

A pay in lieu of notice (PILON) clause: key features, questions and consequences

- It is exercisable at the employer's discretion
- Is pay for the whole or part of the notice period due to the employee?
- Does 'pay' mean just salary or does it also include the value of any benefits?
- Because it makes termination without full notice lawful, the employer can still rely on post-termination restrictions on employee.
- It makes the payment liable to income tax (whereas a payment of compensation in lieu under £30,000 may not be).

Written reasons for dismissal

A dismissed employee with one year's service can request a written statement of the reasons for dismissal to be supplied by the employer within 14 days of the request. This is admissible before an employment tribunal.

An employee dismissed while pregnant or after childbirth, so that her maternity leave period ends, must be provided with written reasons, regardless of her length of service and without request.

The employment tribunal will award two weeks' pay (no statutory maximum on a week's pay is applied) for an unreasonable refusal to supply a statement, or the inadequacy of a statement supplied and may make a declaration of the true reason(s) for dismissal.

Frustration can be frustrating

A contract of employment can be 'frustrated' when an unforeseen event makes the performance of the contract impossible or very different from what had originally been intended. When frustration occurs, the contract ends automatically, without a dismissal. A prison sentence will not necessarily frustrate the contract. A significant factor is the length of the sentence. Where the contract provides for long-term sickness absence, a prison sentence of equivalent length may not be regarded as amounting to frustration. The difficulty is knowing when the point of frustration has been reached. If it has not, but the employer acts as if it has, a dismissal will result. And, it will often be unfair. So, generally, frustration is best left as a legal argument to be deployed in litigation.

Unfair dismissal – General régime

Unless dismissal is found to be for an 'automatically unfair reason (see below opposite), an employee must have been 'continuously employed' for one year at the 'date of dismissal' in order to have protection.

Avoiding the 'one year's service' requirement: dos and don'ts

There are good reasons for giving all employees the same standard of treatment regardless of their length of service. And rushing to beat the 'one year' deadline has its risks. Equally, however, there is little point in an employer allowing a situation to arise which will cost time and money unnecessarily. So, where applicable:

- make a date of termination fall at least one week before the first anniversary of commencement

- provided that the dismissal is not for gross misconduct, terminate immediately with pay in lieu of notice (rather than terminating with actual, working notice)

- phrase letters carefully. For example, make sure that the date of termination is not stated, or represented as, the date on which notice would have expired if it had been given

- ensure that no right of appeal against dismissal preserves employment until the appeal is determined.

'Dismissal'

Dismissal occurs if:

- the employer terminates the contract, with or without notice; or
- a limited-term contract (one whose duration is set by reference to a period of time, the completion of a task or the occurrence or non-occurrence of an event) terminates without renewal; or
- the employer's conduct is a significant breach or repudiation of the employment contract, giving the employee the right to resign with or without notice and the employee exercises this right ('constructive' dismissal).

To establish 'constructive' dismissal, does the employee have to resign without notice?

No. The vital thing is that the employee must, because of the employer's act or omission, have the right to resign without giving notice. If that condition is satisfied, the employee may, in principle, give full notice of resignation and remain working until the specified termination date.

Of course, in many situations of this type, that approach is not a practical one and not in the interests of either party.

Also, if an employee did give notice and remain at work through the notice period, the (ex-) employer may well be able, in any subsequent tribunal proceedings, to draw inferences from the employee's behaviour. Is it an indication that the conduct stated to have caused the resignation did not occur? Or was it in fact not serious enough to give the employee the right to resign immediately and so to be the basis of a 'constructive' dismissal?

Common misconception (4)

'...A constructive dismissal will always be unfair'

Not so. Strictly, establishing a 'constructive' dismissal does no more than confirm that there has been a dismissal – its fairness is a separate matter.

So, while almost all constructive dismissals based on inter-personal behaviour or attitude will end up as unfair, some derived from the breach of express contractual terms can be found to be fair.

For example, an imposed significant reduction of an employee's pay will be a breach of contract that entitles the employee to resign without notice. But, if the employer had a good business reason for the change and conducted appropriate consultation first, then the resultant constructive dismissal could well be fair.

Fairness of a dismissal

If an ex-employee complains of unfair dismissal, the employer must show that there was, at the time of the decision to dismiss, a (principal) reason for it. To be admissible, that principal reason must be one of the following:

- capability (performance/skill or health related) or qualifications
- misconduct
- redundancy
- continued employment in that capacity being illegal
- some other substantial reason justifying dismissal
- 'retirement' (specifically defined and regulated).

The employment tribunal must then decide whether, in view of the employer's size and administrative resources, the dismissal was reasonable in all the circumstances. This involves consideration of:

- *the quality of the pre-decision procedure* (including notification of, and formal dialogue with, the employee and sharing of information relevant to the situation). This is necessary unless the employer can safely conclude that the circumstances are such as to make such formalities 'utterly useless'

- *the factual situation or findings.* At the conclusion of the above procedure, were there, given the evidence available, at least reasonable grounds for continuing to consider the employee for dismissal?; and

- *the ultimate choice of the sanction or outcome of dismissal.* Were the factual situation or findings capable of justifying termination, even if some reasonable employers might not have dismissed? Were any reasonable alternatives to dismissal properly considered?

The 'band of reasonableness'

Different employers may adopt different approaches but each may nevertheless act fairly. In all cases 'there is a band of reasonableness within which one employer might reasonably take one view: another quite reasonably take a different view' (Lord Denning in British Leyland v Swift). If a dismissal falls within the band, and a proper procedure has been followed, the employer will have acted reasonably and the dismissal will be fair.

The tests for assessing whether an employer has acted reasonably in dismissing an employee were set out in Iceland Frozen Foods Limited v Jones:

- the starting point is the statutory provision that the employer must have acted reasonably in dismissing the employee
- in applying this statutory provision, the tribunal must consider the reasonableness of the employer's conduct, not simply whether they (the members of the tribunal) consider the dismissal to be fair
- in judging the reasonableness of the employer's conduct, the tribunal must not substitute its view of the right course to adopt for that of the employer
- in many (though not all) cases there is a band of reasonable responses to the employee's conduct within which one employer might reasonably take one view, another quite reasonably take another
- the function of the tribunal, as an industrial jury, is to determine whether in the particular circumstances of each case the decision to dismiss the employee fell within the band of reasonable responses which a reasonable employer might have adopted. If the dismissal falls within the band, the dismissal is fair: if the dismissal falls outside the band, it is unfair.

How will the tribunal assess the fairness of the reason for dismissal?

Depending on the reason for dismissal, the principal relevant factors that the employment tribunal will consider under 'reasonableness' are:

For Capability

- on grounds of performance/skill
  - warnings
  - hearings/appeals
  - targets for improvement
  - assistance/training
  - alternative employment
  - accompaniment (at least, where the performance management has a disciplinary aspect)

- on grounds of health (see also Disability Discrimination Act in Chapter 8)
  - consultation with the employee
  - medical report/information
  - reasonable adjustments/alternative employment
  - hearing/appeal.

For Conduct (disciplinary matters)

- quality of the investigation
- gravity of the situation (previous warnings or gross misconduct)
- notice of charges and provision of evidence to the employee
- ACAS code of practice
- existence and handling of hearing and appeal (including accompaniment)
- the employee's previous disciplinary record
- precedents set in dealing with other employees.

Determining misconduct

Employment tribunals apply a three-stage test in the case of most misconduct dismissals. The employer must show that:

- he believed the employee was guilty of misconduct
- he had in his mind reasonable grounds upon which to sustain that belief
- at the stage at which he formed that belief on those grounds, he had carried out as much investigation into the matter as was reasonable in the circumstances.

This test (the so-called Burchell test) arose from a case of dishonesty. But the principles laid down have become the established test for determining whether the reason for an employer's decision to dismiss was sufficient in other types of conduct case where the employer has no direct proof of the employee's misconduct, but only a strong suspicion.

For Redundancy

- adequacy of consultation
- approach to selection
- consideration and availability of alternative employment.

In cases of redundancy, where selection from a group of employees is necessary, the selection criteria must be objective (Williams v Compair Maxam). That is, they must not simply reflect the personal opinion of the selector, but should be capable of at least some objective assessment and, preferably, supported by data such as attendance and performance records. Imprecise criteria that can be challenged such as employees 'best suited for the needs of the business under the new operating conditions' and 'attitude to work' will not do.

For Illegality

Possible reasons include disqualification from driving, expiry or lack of a work permit and breach of health and safety legislation (there must be definite illegality involved, not just a reasonable belief in it)

- discussion with the employee
- consideration of alternative employment that would not be illegal
- hearing/appeal.

For some other substantial reason

For example, the end of a limited-term contract, a change in the contract of employment or pressure to dismiss from a customer, regulatory body or another employee

- discussion/consultation with the employee
- exploration of compromises or alternative employment opportunities
- hearing/appeal.

Mutual trust and confidence

Breaching the implied term of mutual trust and confidence has given rise to many successful constructive dismissal cases. Failure to redress a grievance is one example.

In W A Goold (Peermak) Limited v McConall and another the Employment Appeal Tribunal agreed with a tribunal's decision that an employer is under an implied duty to 'reasonably and promptly afford a reasonable opportunity to their employees to obtain redress of any grievance they may have'. In this case, the employer failed to deal with the grievance of two sales people whose work methods had been changed, resulting in a reduction of earnings.

For Retirement

If the employer notified the employee in accordance with the procedure provided for by the legislation on age discrimination, the dismissal took effect on the intended date of retirement and was on/after either age 65 (when no normal retirement age) or normal retirement age (which, if below 65, must not be unlawful age discrimination).

- Has the employee been notified, at least 14 days before the intended date of retirement, of the employer's intention that the employee should retire?

- If the employee has requested not to retire, has the employer dealt with the request properly?
- Provided that the retirement procedure is fully observed, it will not be possible for the employee to try to establish that the employer really had another reason or motive for dismissal.

Dismissals connected with a transfer

It is unfair to dismiss an employee for a reason connected with a transfer of an undertaking, whether before or after the transfer, unless:

- there is an economic, technical or organisational reason entailing changes in the workforce. This requires a reduction in numbers or alterations to job content and frequently equates to redundancy
- **and** the dismissal is handled reasonably.

Convicted offenders

It is normally unfair to dismiss for a 'spent' conviction (see Chapter 8)

Unfair dismissal – exceptions to the normal requirement for service

The following reasons for dismissal are not subject to the normal requirement for one year's continuous employment.

It is automatically unfair to dismiss an employee:

- for bringing, or for being involved in, proceedings relating to the enforcement of the National Minimum Wage
- for refusing to work in excess of 48 hours a week or during a rest break
- for signing a workforce agreement or opt out agreement; or for being an 'appropriate representative' or candidate in a workforce agreement on Working Time

- for the following reasons related to a trade union:
  - membership, or participation in activities, of an independent trade union or
  - non-membership of a trade union or
  - involvement in trade union recognition or derecognition
  - refusal of an employer's offer of inducement.

An employer can 'join' (that is, add) a person or trade union or contractor as a party to a claim for unfair dismissal if the employer claims to have been induced to dismiss by a threat of industrial action.

If a union or other person puts pressure on an employer to dismiss by calling or threatening to call industrial action because of an employee's non-membership of a union, the ex-employee can add the union or other person as a party to unfair dismissal proceedings.

- for the following reasons related to maternity:
  - pregnancy
  - giving birth
  - taking ordinary or additional maternity leave or receiving benefits during ordinary maternity leave
  - being subject to a requirement or recommendation to suspend work on health and safety grounds
- for reasons related to taking, or seeking to take, paternity leave, adoption leave, or paternity leave on adoption
- for exercising, or seeking to exercise, the right to request flexible working, or for accompanying, or seeking to accompany, an employee who wishes to exercise this right
- for the following reasons related to parental leave:
  - taking or seeking to take parental leave
  - declining to sign a workforce agreement on parental leave
  - being an appropriate representative or candidate in a workforce agreement on parental leave
- for seeking to take or taking time off to care for dependants
- for exercising rights under the part-time workers regulations
- for exercising rights under the fixed-term employees regulations
- for exercising or seeking to exercise the right to be accompanied at a hearing, to have a meeting rescheduled, or to be accompanied by or to seek to accompany another worker
- for exercising rights concerned with health and safety (see Chapter 7)
- who is an employee representative or candidate, for performing, or proposing to perform, relevant functions as such
- who is a trustee of an occupational pension scheme, for performing, or proposing to perform, relevant functions or activities as such
- who is a protected or opted-out shop worker or betting worker, for refusing or threatening to refuse to work on a Sunday or any shop worker for opting-out or proposing to do so

- for being summoned or being absent to attend jury service unless:
  - the absence was likely to cause substantial injury to the employer's undertaking; and
  - being aware of that, the employee unreasonably failed to apply to be excused from jury service
- for making a protected disclosure ('whistleblowing') in the public interest
- for asserting (to an employment tribunal or employer) an employment protection right available under the Employment Rights Act or, in some cases, the Trade Union and Labour Relations (Consolidation) Act. It is irrelevant that the employee is not, in fact, qualified for that right or that the right has not been infringed, provided that the claim is made in good faith
- on grounds of sex, race, disability, sexual orientation, religion, belief or age because that is an unlawful act under one of those separate pieces of legislation
- for taking, or having taken, part in official (authorised or endorsed by a trade union – see Chapter 14) and lawful ('protected' by statutory immunities – see Chapter 14) industrial action in one of the following circumstances:
- during the twelve-week, 'protected period' starting with the first day on which the action was taken by the employee
- after the twelve-week period, but when the employee's participation in the action stopped before the end of that period
- when the employee's action continued beyond the twelve-week period, but the employer had not followed all reasonable procedural steps to resolve the dispute.

And also note:

1 The fairness of a dismissal **occurring during participation** in official industrial action that is not lawful will not be considered by a tribunal unless some other participants were not dismissed at the time, or although all were originally dismissed at that time, some were re-engaged within a period of three months.

2 Those dismissed **at the time of their participation** in 'unofficial' industrial action have no right to claim unfair dismissal.

3 Those dismissed for **having previously** taken industrial action of the types described in 1 and 2 above retain the right to bring a claim for 'general' unfair dismissal.

Remedies for unfair dismissal

On a finding of unfair dismissal, an employment tribunal must consider reinstatement (same employment) and re-engagement (comparable or suitable employment) and must first ask whether the ex-employee wants one of these solutions. Practicability is relevant, but not the engagement of a 'permanent' replacement, unless this was the only sensible way of getting work done.

Unless it is not practicable for the employer to comply, punitive compensation (known as an 'additional award') can be awarded for the employer's refusal to comply with a reinstatement/re-engagement order. This compensation will be between 26 and 52 weeks' pay (maximum of £380 per week with effect from 1st October 2009).

Also, in all cases, the tribunal will award standard unfair dismissal compensation.

Standard compensation for unfair dismissal

This normally takes the form of a two-part award:

Basic award

This is calculated in the same way as a statutory redundancy payment but:

- £4,700 is the minimum for dismissal for:
  - non-membership of a union
  - union membership or activities
  - undertaking activities in connection with reducing risks to health and safety, having been designated by the employer to undertake such activities
  - performing functions as a designated safety representative or member of a safety committee
  - for 'employee representative' or 'pension trustee' reasons
- 4 weeks' pay (maximum of £1,520 with effect from October 2009) is the minimum award for procedurally unfair dismissal for 'retirement'.

Compensatory award

This seeks to reflect the employee's true financial loss, including pensions and estimated future loss. The current maximum is £65,300 (with effect from 1st February 2010). The award is unlimited for health and safety, public interest disclosure and sex, race and disability age/religion/sexual orientation discrimination dismissals.

A tribunal may order a discretionary increase of up to 25% for the failure by an employer to follow the guidance set out in the ACAS Code of Practice 1 on disciplinary and grievance procedures, although the cap on the compensatory award still applies for unfair dismissal.

A tribunal may also order a discretionary reduction of up to 25% for the failure by an employee to follow the ACAS guidance.

The limits on the awards are normally reviewed annually, for implementation from February.

The compensatory award can be reduced by the tribunal if:

- the ex-employee has unreasonably failed to seek or take up work elsewhere (breach of the duty to mitigate loss) and/or has been guilty of conduct contributing to the dismissal (this also applies to the basic award); and/or
- the ex-employee could have been fairly dismissed for something discovered soon after dismissal (and before the tribunal hearing); and/or
- the tribunal believes the dismissal would still have occurred if required procedures had been observed and, in those circumstances, the dismissal would have been fair.

A reduction on any of these grounds is considered from the starting point of an employee's full calculated loss before the statutory cap mentioned above is applied.

Interim relief

This is an order by the tribunal for the contract of employment to continue until a decision on the complaint of unfair dismissal has been reached. Ex-employees can apply for this relief if they claim they have been unfairly dismissed for:

- non-membership of a union
- union membership or activities
- undertaking activities in connection with reducing risks to health and safety, having been designated by the employer to undertake such activities
- performing functions as a designated safety representative or member of a safety committee
- for 'employees' representative' or 'pension trustee' reasons.

11. Redundancy payments

11 Redundancy payments

The right is to a lump-sum compensation payment for an employee who fulfils the prescribed conditions and is:

- dismissed because of redundancy or
- laid-off, or kept on short time within the contract, for several weeks.

Conditions for eligibility

- The employee must have continuous service of at least two years.
- There must be a dismissal (unless the specific provisions on lay-off and short-time apply). For this purpose, 'dismissal' has the same definition as that used for unfair dismissal.

Dismissal for redundancy

Termination of employment will be 'by reason of redundancy' if:

- the employer has ceased, or intends to cease, to carry on the business, overall or in a particular place where the employee works or is based, or
- the employer's requirement for employees to do 'work of a particular kind' has ceased or diminished, or is expected to cease or diminish, overall or in a particular place where the employee works or is based.

Common misconception (5)

'...there must be a net reduction in jobs for the redundancy definition to be satisfied'

That is often the case, but it is not necessary. The same number of jobs might be transferred to a new location from a closing one, or even more new jobs might be created at the new location: redundancy would still apply to those employees whose place of work was closing.

Furthermore, the second limb of the redundancy definition refers to the requirement for a particular type of work to have ceased or diminished. Sometimes, at the same location, an employer will make changes in the content of jobs (even though they may retain the same title). And that employer may be content for the people in the 'old' jobs to continue in the new or reconfigured ones. But there may then be an argument that the extent of the change in job content is such as to make the latest requirement one for work of a new, different kind. Any termination would then be by reason of redundancy and give rise to eligibility for a statutory payment.

Possible disqualification from entitlement to a redundancy payment

An employee's entitlement to a redundancy payment is only maintained if the employee does not unreasonably refuse any offer of suitable alternative work that the employer makes before the ending of the contract for the redundant job. For this purpose:

- an offer on the same terms in the same place disqualifies the employee from payment
- an offer on different terms or in a different place raises questions of flexibility, suitability, and the reasonableness of refusal.

There is provision for a trial period of at least four weeks in any new job that is offered. The expiry of the trial period is regarded as acceptance of the new job.

If, during the trial period, the employee terminates the employment for whatever reason, or the employer terminates it for a reason arising out of the change, then the employee is treated for redundancy payment purposes as dismissed from the original job. The employee therefore receives a redundancy payment, unless the new job was suitable and termination unreasonable. However, even then, the dismissal may still be unfair according to the considerations mentioned previously (see Chapter 10).

Common misconception (6)

'...the conditions governing entitlement to a statutory redundancy payment also apply to access to an additional 'company' redundancy payment'

Formally, they do not. When an employment tribunal applies the rules in the Employment Rights Act, it can only make a decision that is binding on the parties in relation to a statutory payment. The entitlement to an enhanced payment, whether introduced in the contract of employment or in negotiation or consultation under a specific redundancy exercise, does not automatically follow.

That said, if there are no separate detailed rules in place, it will be difficult to resist practical and legal pressure to treat the additional payment component in the same way as the statutory. So, if it is intended to depart from the criteria used for the statutory scheme, it is sensible for an enhanced scheme explicitly to set down its own rules and conditions.

For example, it might provide that refusal of any offer of alternative employment (not just 'suitable' alternative employment) disqualifies an employee from the non-statutory payment.

Lay-off and short-time

An employee can claim a redundancy payment if laid off or on short time for four consecutive weeks, or for a broken series of six weeks in any thirteen:

- lay-off is no work and no pay of any kind from the employer for the week in question
- short time is shortage of work and less than half pay for that week.

Note: the statutory provisions on guarantee payments (see Chapter 4) use a different definition of lay-off, based on individual workless days.

The employee must initiate the process by giving the employer, within 4 weeks of latest week of lay-off or short time, written notice of intention to claim a redundancy payment.

Entitlement then depends on whether the employer serves counter-notice within seven days, contesting the claim because there is a reasonable prospect of a sustained resumption. If so, the employment tribunal decides. Payment, in any event, is made only when the employee resigns with notice.

The service requirement of two years applies. This statutory right is only needed where the contract of employment allows the employer to lay the employee off and/or to implement short time. Without this right the employee would be unable to claim a redundancy payment, regardless of the length of the lay-off or short time.

If the contract does not contain lay-off/short-time provisions, an employee experiencing lay-off or short time can resign and assert 'constructive' dismissal by reason of redundancy in order to get a statutory payment.

Calculation of a statutory redundancy payment

The calculation is based on a scale, working back from the date of dismissal:

- for each year of reckonable service from age 41 — 1½ week's pay
- for each year of reckonable service from age 22 to 40 — 1 week's pay
- for each year of reckonable service below age 22 — ½ week's pay

A 'week's pay' is calculated according to defined rules.

Applicable limits:

- the maximum service taken into account is 20 years (a 'year' being 12 complete calendar months)
- with effect from 1st October 2009, the maximum 'one week's pay' is £380 and the maximum payment is £11,400.

The maximum amount of 'one week's pay' (and therefore of a statutory redundancy payment) is normally reviewed annually.

'Indirect' age discrimination and redundancy payments

Although it is, in part, based on length of service, the statutory redundancy payment scheme is specifically exempted by legislation from any unlawfulness caused by 'indirect' age discrimination.

Any scheme for enhanced redundancy payments will also be completely exempt from such unlawfulness provided that it uses the statutory scheme's classification of ages and bases itself on the same sliding scale of 'weeks' pay' entitlement (see above: Calculation of a redundancy payment) before applying a common multiplier or ignoring the maximum on a week's pay.

Any other form of service-based enhanced scheme will need to satisfy the 'objective justification' test under age discrimination legislation.

Claims for redundancy payments

A claim for a redundancy payment must be made within six months of the termination of the contract (unless a claim for unfair dismissal is made within three months). The employment tribunal can hear a time-barred claim within a further six months, if that is just and equitable in the circumstances.

If the tribunal awards an ex-employee a statutory redundancy payment, it may also award compensation for any financial loss caused by the employer's non-payment.

Consultation on and notification of large-scale redundancies

There is a duty to consult representatives of employees (see Chapter 12).

At the same time as representatives are being consulted, there is also a duty to notify the Department for Business Innovation and Skills (DBIS) on Form HR1 of the proposed number of redundancies. Failure to notify can result in criminal proceedings and a fine not exceeding £5,000 against the company and/or officer.

Unfair dismissal and redundancy

A dismissal for redundancy may be unfair on grounds that:

- the employer has failed to give the employee as much warning or opportunity for one-to-one consultation as is reasonably practicable (unless the employer can reasonably conclude, at the time, that such consultation would be futile); or
- the selection criteria used are unreasonable in themselves or have been applied unreasonably; or
- the employer has failed to consider and, if appropriate, offer the employee any alternative employment that was available.

Common misconception (7)

'...the employer's duty to consider and explore with the employee opportunities for alternative employment only extends to work that is suitable'

Unfair dismissal law focuses on what reasonable measures the employer has taken to avoid the dismissal of an employee whose current job is redundant. Unemployment, even temporary, is undesirable, both for the individual and for society.

So, the employer's duty covers most, if not all opportunities or vacancies that exist within the organisation, regardless of their nature, worth or status. It is the employee's prerogative to refuse on one or more of these grounds, but not the employer's right to forego at least discussing them with the employee.

Of course, in the context of entitlement to a statutory redundancy payment, the employee's refusal of a 'suitable' alternative job may have consequences. But that is a different matter, based on a separate set of rules.

Also, a redundancy dismissal will not be justified if the employee is selected for any of the 'automatically unfair' reasons referred to in Chapter 10. The normal service qualification for unfair dismissal does not apply to these automatically unfair reasons.

12. Consultation with employees' representatives

12 Consultation with employees' representatives

Redundancy

Basic obligation

An employer must consult with 'appropriate representatives' of employees if it is proposing to dismiss as redundant 20 or more employees at one establishment within a period of 90 days or less.

'Establishment'

This is defined as the 'unit' to which the workers at risk of redundancy are 'assigned'.

An 'establishment' can consist of several workplaces at separate physical locations. Conversely, it is possible to have two establishments based at the same site. An establishment can exist even where the affected workers do not have a specific, 'physical' workplace provided by the employer at all (for example, sales representatives).

'Redundant' and 'proposing to dismiss'

The definition of 'redundant' is broader than that used for redundancy payment purposes. It covers any reason 'not related to the individual' – so it extends to proposed changes in terms and conditions and/or working arrangements that do not eliminate posts (reduce the staff) or alter the essential nature of jobs.

And, whatever types of 'redundancy' are involved in an exercise, the question whether an employer is 'proposing to dismiss' employees has to be answered by reference to what might be necessary. For example, an employer might hope, often justifiably, that there will be sufficient volunteers to meet the targeted reduction or that employees will agree to changes in terms and conditions. But, if those hopes are not borne out, the desired results would require the termination of existing contracts of employment (a 'dismissal'). That possibility must be taken into account in counting (for the purpose of the 20+ threshold) the number of employees affected.

Employees' representatives

'Appropriate representatives' are representatives of a recognised trade union or representatives elected by the employees.

If there is a recognised trade union for some or all categories of affected employees, the employer must consult only its representatives about those employees affected by the redundancy and who are covered by trade union recognition.

There is a loosely-prescribed method for electing employees' representatives.

Timescales

Consultation must begin 'in good time' and, if at least 20 redundancies are proposed, no less than 30 days or, for 100 or more redundancies, no less than 90 days before the first redundancy dismissal is due to take effect.

Preliminary information that must be provided to the representatives

Initial written notification to appropriate representatives must provide information about the reasons for the proposed redundancies, the numbers and descriptions of the employees affected, the proposed selection procedures, the proposed method of carrying out the dismissals, including the period over which they are to take effect, and the proposed method of calculating any non-statutory redundancy payments.

Scope of consultation

Consultation with representatives must be with a view to reaching agreement and must cover ways of:

- avoiding dismissals
- reducing the number of dismissals
- reducing the effects of dismissals.

The first two subjects for consultation mean that it may also be necessary for the employer to consult about the business or organisational plan that has resulted in the proposal for redundancies.

Fair and complete collective consultation

Fair consultation about redundancy means consultation when the proposals are still at a formative stage. It 'involves giving the body consulted a fair and proper opportunity to understand fully the matters about which it is being consulted, and to express its views on those subjects, with the consultor thereafter considering those views properly and genuinely' (Lord Glidewell).

The European Court of Justice has said that an employer may not terminate any contracts of employment or issue notices of dismissal until the process of collective consultation has been completed. But this does not mean that 30, or as the case may be, 90 days' consultation must have expired. It is possible to agree that collective consultation has been completed before this or for it to have run its course even though there is no agreement.

Consequence of non-compliance

Failure to consult gives rise to a complaint to the employment tribunal and to possible protective awards of up to 90 days' pay per employee affected by the failure (whether yet made redundant or not).

The maximum award is the starting point for the tribunal: a lesser amount will only be awarded if there are mitigating circumstances surrounding the employer's non-compliance.

Transfer of Undertakings

Basic duty and timing

The employer's obligations to consult arise before a 'relevant transfer' of a business or undertaking. For this and the effect of the transfer regulations on individual contracts of employees in a business/undertaking, see Chapter 9.

The duty is initially to provide information, in writing, to appropriate representatives (see above) of 'affected employees' long enough before the transfer to allow any necessary consultation to occur.

'Affected employees' of the existing organisation (transferor) or the incoming organisation (transferee) are those who may be affected by the transfer or by measures taken in connection with the transfer.

Information to be provided

The required information is:

- reasons for the transfer and its approximate timing
- the legal, economic and social implications of the transfer
- the measures envisaged by the employer or the fact that no measures are envisaged
- in the case of the transferor, the measures that it envisages the transferee will take with the transferred employees. Or, if it envisages that no measures will be taken, that fact.

Possible duty to consult

The duty of those employers who do envisage taking any pre-transfer measures with their own employees is then to consult with representatives with a view to reaching agreement on them.

No minimum timescale for commencing such consultation is set down, unless the measure is 'redundancy' and the numbers and timescales bring into play the need to consult representatives of employees about redundancies (see above).

If a transferee envisages making redundancies after the transfer, that measure is subject to consultation with employees' representatives only once the transferee has become the employer and only if the proposed redundancies in an establishment number at least 20 and will occur within 90 days or less.

Consequence of non-compliance

Failure to inform or, if applicable, to consult gives rise to a complaint to the employment tribunal and possible compensation (of up to 13 weeks' pay, with no statutory cap) to each employee affected.

The transferee is jointly and severally liable with the transferor in respect of other awards of compensation against the transferor arising from a failure to inform or consult.

However, if the transferor's breach arises from the transferee's failure to give the transferor information about the proposed measures, compensation is normally payable by the transferee.

Health and safety

There is an obligation on the employer to consult representatives of employees (or employees individually) on certain health and safety matters.

General workplace information and consultation

The Information and Consultation with Employees Regulations apply to undertakings with 50 or more employees in the UK.

The employer's obligation to consult arises only after a 'trigger' request. Should employees make a valid request, employers are under an obligation to establish means for information and consultation to give the employees a better idea of potential changes in their employment.

To be valid, a request must be made in writing by 10% of the employees in the undertaking, subject to a minimum of 15 employees and a maximum of 2,500 employees.

Negotiation and voluntary and pre-existing agreements

Following the receipt of a request, and subject to the provisions about a pre-existing agreement (see below), the employer has six months (extendable by agreement) in which to negotiate a voluntary agreement with the employees' representatives.

If a voluntary agreement is reached, it must:

- set out the circumstances in which the employer will inform and consult the employees

- provide either for dealing with the employees' representatives or for the information and consultation to be directly with employees (or both)
- be recorded in writing and dated
- cover all of the employees in the undertaking
- be signed by the employer and approved by the employees.

The regulations provide for the possible retention of any pre-existing agreements endorsed by the workforce. A valid pre-existing agreement must:

- be in writing
- cover all the employees in the undertaking
- set out how the employer will inform and consult the employees
- be approved by the employees.

If the employer already has a pre-existing agreement in place when it receives a valid request, it may ballot the workforce to seek endorsement of the request. If, after a ballot, a minimum of 40% of the employees (constituting a majority of those who actually voted) endorses the request, the pre-existing agreement becomes invalid and negotiation on a voluntary agreement must commence.

Standard, default provisions

If no voluntary agreement is reached by negotiation, 'standard' provisions will apply. This will require the establishment of an information and consultation committee, representing all employees in the undertaking, after the election of representatives. The number of representatives is proportional to the number of employees (one representative for every 50 employees up to a maximum of 25 representatives).

The standard provisions require the employer to inform and consult the employees and to provide:

- information on the recent and probable development of the undertaking's activities and economic situation
- information and consultation on the situation, structure and probable development of employment within the undertaking and on any anticipatory measures envisaged, particularly if there is a threat to employment within the undertaking

- information and consultation, with a view to reaching agreement, on decisions likely to lead to substantial changes in work organisation or in contractual relations between the employer and its employees. These include decisions entailing collective redundancies and business transfers – areas that are covered by separate obligations to consult employees' representatives.

Subsequent requests from employees

If the employees have made a request, or negotiations have been initiated by the employer, no further request may be made for three years after the conclusion of a negotiated agreement or the application of the standard provisions.

Consequence of non-compliance

If an employer has failed to establish arrangements for information and consultation, an employee may complain to the Central Arbitration Committee (CAC). The CAC will deal with any disputes about the operation of such arrangements. Sanctions for employers involve a range of remedies based on orders to perform obligations under the legislation and financial penalties of up to £75,000, depending on the size of the employer and other factors. If the CAC upholds a complaint that bears a financial penalty against an employer, an employee may make an application to the Employment Appeal Tribunal for payment.

Pension matters

The duty to consult on pensions is on a 'relevant employer' with 50 or more employees.

A 'relevant employer' is one operating or participating in an occupational pension scheme (other than a small or public service scheme) or a personal pension scheme with the employer's contributions.

The duty to consult covers a 'listed change' to future arrangements under the applicable scheme.

Listed changes for occupational schemes:

- raising the pension age
- closing the scheme to new members
- stopping future accruals
- ceasing the employer's contributions
- introducing or increasing the member's contributions
- reducing the employer's contributions (money purchase only)
- converting to money purchase (defined benefit only)
- changing the basis of future accrual (defined benefit only).

Listed changes for personal schemes:

- removing or reducing the employer's contributions
- increasing the members' contributions.

If the trustees or managers of a scheme instigate the listed change, they must notify the relevant employer(s) in writing.

Each employer must provide written information to those employees who are 'affected members' and any existing appropriate representatives of such people.

The information for 'affected members' must include:

- a description of the change and its likely effects,
- appropriate background information and
- an indication of timescale.

Existing 'appropriate representatives' are those:

- of a recognised trade union,
- elected or appointed under a negotiated voluntary agreement or 'standard' arrangement under information and consultation regulations,
- under pre-existing agreement for purposes of the information and consultation regulations, or
- previously elected for purposes of occupational and personal pension scheme regulations.

Subsequent consultation by the employer must be with:

- one or more of the types of existing appropriate representative above and/or (if a pre-existing or negotiated agreement under the information and consultation regulations provides for direct consultation with employees) with the affected members directly; or
- if existing representatives or direct consultation arrangements do not exist or do not cover some or all affected members:
- representatives newly elected for purposes of occupational and personal pension schemes regulations; or
- if no such representatives are elected for some or all affected members, those affected members directly.

The consultation period

This must be at least 60 days. At its outset, an employer may specify the date for the end of consultation or for the submission of written responses.

If no responses are submitted by a specified end-date, the consultation is complete. If responses are received, the employer must consider them before deciding whether to make the proposed change. For this purpose, if the employer was not the initiator of the proposal for change, it must pass such responses to the initiator.

Enforcement

This is by a complaint to the Pensions Regulator, who can order the payment of a 'civil penalty' of up to £50,000 for a breach (but the Regulator cannot order the reversal of the relevant change).

13. The Employment Tribunal: System and process

13 The Employment Tribunal: System and process

Composition

Normally the employment tribunal has three members: the Employment Judge (a qualified lawyer) and two lay members, one with managerial or business experience and one with experience of representing employees. A majority decision is possible.

The Employment Judge may sit alone on certain matters or with the consent of the parties.

Representation

A party may choose not to be represented but to conduct its own case. If representation is desired, it need not be by a lawyer. Legal aid is not available (except in Scotland).

Steps before a hearing:

- the employee or ex-employee (claimant) completes the claim form (Form ET1) and lodges it, normally within three months, with the tribunal
- the tribunal serves a copy on the employer (respondent) and notifies ACAS
- the employer has 28 days to enter a response (Form ET3). If this time limit (or any extended limit agreed by the tribunal) is not complied with, the tribunal will normally issue a 'default judgment', finding in favour of the claimant
- ACAS assigns a conciliation officer to promote a settlement without the need for a hearing.

Settling a claim

There are two legally valid ways of settling a claim – a settlement drawn up after conciliation by ACAS or a compromise agreement.

Conciliation

In conciliation, the ACAS officer has no duty of confidentiality to the parties and cannot advise them on the merits of their cases.

Any settlement reached is recorded on a Form COT3 and signed by both parties or their authorised representatives. In addition to specifying the core agreement, the settlement will usually include a time limit for payment of any agreed sum and may feature obligations on other subjects, such as the provision of a reference and the maintenance of confidentiality.

Compromise agreement

This is reached directly, without the assistance of ACAS, between the employer and the employee. The parties must be advised beforehand by a 'relevant independent adviser' (a qualified lawyer or, with certified competence, a trade union official or advice worker).

To be legally effective, a compromise agreement must be in writing, specify the claim(s) or proceedings it covers, identify the adviser (who must have appropriate insurance cover) and explicitly confirm that these conditions have been met.

Employment disputes that have not yet resulted in a claim to the tribunal can also be conclusively settled either through ACAS conciliation or by a compromise agreement.

Processing a claim

There are four types of hearing: pre-hearing review; case management discussion; full hearing; and review hearing.

A pre-hearing review can consider preliminary points (see below) and/or the merits of the case. The tribunal may rule that a claim is inadmissible or, if it has no reasonable prospect of success, strike it out. It may also require the claimant to pay a deposit to be allowed to continue (maximum £500).

The powers of the Employment Tribunal

Before the case is fully heard, the tribunal, often at a case management discussion (which is sometimes done by telephone), may direct either or both parties:

- to provide further particulars of the case
- to give relevant documents (or copies) to the other party, and/or
- to exchange written statements of the evidence of each witness who will appear at the full hearing.

Failure to comply with an order can result in the case being struck out and/or the party being fined.

The tribunal can also order the attendance of a witness. Disobedience without excuse can result in the witness being fined.

Preliminary points

In order to give the tribunal jurisdiction to hear the case, the claimant may need to prove (if any of these matters is disputed) that he or she:

- is or was an employee of or worker for that employer
- is protected – not one of the excluded classes (such as Crown employees, police and mariners)
- is qualified to complain (that the time limit has not been exceeded)
- was dismissed – if applicable.

There is often a separate, pre-hearing review to consider one or more of these points. Evidence from witnesses on those points is permitted.

Procedure (for pre-hearing reviews and full hearings)

The party under the burden of proof starts by giving evidence through relevant witnesses (who take the oath or affirm) and supporting documentation. Each witness is open to cross-examination by the other side and to questioning by the tribunal. The same process applies when the other party in turn presents its case.

On completion of the evidence, each party makes a closing statement to the tribunal (the party under the burden of proof goes second).

The employment tribunal may give a decision on the day or later (a reserved decision). It may be unanimous or by a majority. It is always provided in writing, in either full/extended form (which is mandatory in discrimination cases) or in brief/summary form.

Challenging a decision

Review hearing

This may be requested by a party who believes that the employment tribunal itself should reconsider its decision because of:

- an administrative error
- the party's non-receipt of notice of hearing
- the making of the decision despite the justified absence of the party
- the availability of new evidence
- 'the interests of justice'.

Appeals

These can be made, on points of law only, to the Employment Appeal Tribunal and upwards to the Court of Appeal (or, in Scotland, the Court of Session) and the Supreme Court.

Referral to the European Court of Justice

This may be possible for a ruling on the scope and interpretation of EU Directives and their effect on UK legislation.

Litigation in the 'ordinary' courts

These are the County Court, the High Court, the Court of Appeal and the Supreme Court. Employment disputes that are based exclusively on the contract of employment (as opposed to rights created by employment legislation) are sometimes heard by these courts as an alternative or sometimes as a practical necessity. For example, an employment tribunal can only hear claims for breach of contract if they are on termination of employment and can only award a maximum of £25,000.

14. Collective labour law

14 Collective labour law

Recognition of trade unions

Recognition of a trade union is about the employer's acceptance of that union's right to participate in 'collective bargaining' on behalf of, and otherwise to represent the interests of, a category of workers.

Whether an employer chooses voluntarily to recognise a trade union or not, a trade union can nonetheless seek statutory recognition for 'collective bargaining'.

What is 'collective bargaining'?

The scope of collective bargaining will often vary according to the way in which the right to undertake it has arisen in the first place.

If recognition has been voluntarily agreed, collective bargaining can, according to the particular agreement, cover any of the matters under the definition in the Trade Union and Labour Relations (Consolidation) Act. These are:

- terms and conditions of employment
- physical conditions of work
- engagement or non-engagement of any worker
- termination or suspension of employment, or the duties, of any worker
- allocation of work or duties between workers or groups of workers
- disciplinary matters
- a worker's membership or non-membership of a trade union
- facilities for union officials
- the machinery for negotiation and consultation and procedures on the topics above.

When statutory recognition (see below) is awarded, the scope is then either dependent upon the agreement reached ('semi-voluntary') or, if the statutory default model is imposed, it is limited to collective bargaining on:

- pay
- holidays
- hours.

Effects of collective agreements

Incorporation of a collective agreement into the employment contract is the way in which a change agreed by a trade union recognised as having bargaining rights on behalf of an employee becomes legally effective. The making of the new agreement can vary the terms of employment, whether or not the employee is a member of the union. Even if the employment contract does not have an express clause incorporating the results of collective bargaining, the employee is generally treated as having agreed, by entering into the contract, to be bound by terms agreed between the employer and the union.

Legal consequences of recognition

However it comes about, once the recognition of a trade union is established or acknowledged, it brings into being certain rights and responsibilities created by legislation. The major ones concern:

- time off for officials, learning representatives and employees
- consultation on redundancy, measures in connection with a transfer of undertaking and, perhaps, pension changes
- the disclosure of information.

Although these subjects might also be covered by aspects of an initial or subsequent agreement between employer and union, the relevant legislation applies automatically and cannot be excluded by the terms of an agreement or by the failure of an agreement to mention them.

There are other union-related rights that do not depend upon recognition. For example, protection against victimisation and the right to be accompanied at disciplinary and grievance hearings.

'Compulsory' statutory recognition

The statutory recognition procedure allows an independent trade union to seek recognition for collective bargaining on behalf of a specified group of workers. This group of workers is known as the 'bargaining unit'.

The union starts the process by making a written request to the employer for recognition. If voluntary agreement cannot be reached between the parties within a specified period, the union may apply to the CAC to decide on recognition.

What is the procedure if the parties cannot agree?

If the parties cannot agree, within a fixed period, on the appropriate bargaining unit for the debate on recognition, the CAC's first task will be to decide that question.

For an application to proceed, at least 10% of the proposed bargaining unit must be members of the union and, in the view of the CAC, a majority of the workers in the unit must be likely to favour recognition.

If the majority of the workers in the bargaining unit are members of the union, the CAC normally awards recognition without a ballot of the workforce. If a ballot is necessary, recognition must be supported by a majority of those who vote and by at least 40% of the workers who constitute the bargaining unit.

If recognition is granted, the parties must then seek to agree on a method of conducting collective bargaining. If the parties cannot reach agreement, they must adopt the CAC's procedure, which requires the employer to negotiate with the union at least on pay (excluding pension rights), hours and holidays. This enforced agreement will be legally binding between the parties.

Should either the employer or the union fail to comply with a bargaining procedure imposed by the CAC, the offended party can apply to a civil court for an order that the other party comply. Breach of such an order is a criminal offence.

If the application for recognition fails?

Should the application to the CAC ultimately fail (after being allowed to proceed), no further application can be made by the union in respect of the same or similar bargaining unit within the following three years.

There is a similar procedure, to be used in defined circumstances by employer and/or worker, for de-recognition of a union.

Where TUPE applies

Recognition (whether voluntary or statutory) will pass over to the new employer if the transferred entity remains distinct from the rest of the new employer's business.

Disclosure of information

The employer must disclose certain information to recognised independent trades union(s) for collective bargaining. The union(s) must make, and co-ordinate, requests in writing and specify their relevance. There are limitations on the employer's obligations. The ACAS Code of Practice 'Disclosure of Information to Trade Unions for Collective Bargaining Purposes' provides guidance on the disclosure of information. Failure to observe the Code does not itself render anyone liable to proceedings, but relevant provisions of the Code are taken into account in proceedings before the CAC.

The sanction is a complaint to the CAC, which can make 'one-off' awards in individual contracts, based on what the settlement would have been had information been available to the trades union.

Union membership or recognition in commercial contracts

Any term in a commercial contract that specifies the use of only union or non-union labour is void. It is also unlawful to exclude a tender, or to fail to award a contract, or to terminate a contract, on grounds that anyone employed, or likely to be employed, on work connected with the contract is, or is not, a member of a union. The same conditions apply to contracts that specify recognition of and negotiation/consultation with unions or unions' officials.

Industrial action

Industrial action by workers, whether official (supported by one or more trade unions) or not, almost invariably involves, or causes, breaches of contract or other interference with contractual relations. Such breaches or interference may relate to:

- the contracts of employment of those taking the industrial action, and/or
- the contracts of employment of other workers, whether employed by the employer at the heart of the industrial dispute or another caught up in it, and/or
- commercial contracts of the employer at the heart of the dispute or another organisation.

What is the legal position of someone who organises industrial action?

Just as a breach of contract itself can be the subject of a common law legal action by the injured party, so can the civil wrong of inducing or encouraging that breach be the subject of legal action. In legal terms, that is what the organiser of industrial action (whether a union or an individual) does.

It is often more effective for an employer to seek legal redress from an organiser of industrial action, particularly a trade union, than from individual workers.

As a result of the above, leaving the common law to operate by itself would mean that industrial action would almost always be unlawful and open to legal action, regardless of the circumstances. Legislation has therefore intervened to give organiser(s) of the industrial action protection from legal liability if it is 'in contemplation or furtherance of a trade dispute' and also satisfies the requirements of 2 – 7 below.

The statutory immunities of the organiser(s) of industrial action

1 *Definition of trade dispute.* A trade dispute is lawful when workers are in dispute with their own employer and the dispute is wholly or mainly about matters such as pay, conditions and jobs. This excludes disputes between union(s) and employer when none of that employer's employees is in dispute; disputes between unions or groups of workers; and, usually, disputes relating to matters overseas.

2 *Ballots.* A trade union loses immunity if its industrial action is not supported by a ballot. Normally, if industrial action covers different places of work, separate ballots must be held for each one. The employer must have received at least seven days' notice of the union's intention to hold a ballot and must have had sight of the ballot paper at least three days in advance of the ballot. After the ballot, the union must notify the employer

of the result as soon as practicable. Ballots with a potential constituency in excess of 50 must also have an independent scrutineer.

A supporting Code of Practice, 'Industrial Action Ballots and Notice to Employers', provides practical guidance.

3 *Notice and commencement of industrial action.* A trade union must also give the employer(s) subject to industrial action at least seven days' written notice of the start of that action. Failure to do so results in loss of immunity.

Industrial action must start within four weeks (or a longer agreed period not exceeding eight weeks) of the date of the ballot.

The supporting Code of Practice referred to in 2 above provides practical guidance.

4 *Secondary action,* such as blacking and sympathetic strikes, has no immunity, unless it occurs in the course of picketing that is lawful under 7 below.

5 *A person who induces,* or threatens to induce, a breach of contract because the employer employs, or has employed, non-union members or fails, or has failed, to discriminate against them has no immunity.

6 *Pressure to impose membership or recognition of a union(s).* Unions or other persons who organise industrial action to put pressure on an employer to act in a way that is contrary to the provisions in relation to union membership or recognition in commercial contracts (see above) have no immunity from legal action. Nor do those who organise or threaten industrial action that interferes with the supply of goods or services on grounds that:

- work done in connection with the supply of goods or services has been or is likely to be done by non-union members or
- the supplier of the goods and services does not recognise or negotiate/consult with unions or union officials.

7 *Picketing.* Lawful picketing is limited to:

- employees at or near their own place of work
- a union's official accompanying a union member whom he or she represents at or near the member's place of work
- an unemployed person at a former place of work in furtherance of a dispute connected with dismissal, resignation or redundancy.

If it is induced by lawful picketing, secondary action will have immunity from liability – for example, if a delivery driver is persuaded to turn back, so inducing a breach of the driver's contract and of the commercial contract(s) for supply and delivery.

A supporting Code of Practice, 'Picketing', provides practical guidance.

8 *Liability of trades unions.* Those who suffer, or stand to suffer, loss because of unlawful industrial action (action that does not meet the applicable requirements of 2 to 7 above) can seek a court order (injunction) requiring the union to restrain or delay the action and/or can sue the union for damages.

The union is responsible if its actions are authorised or endorsed by the executive committee, president, general secretary or any official (including a shop steward) or committee. If authorisation or endorsement is by an official or committee, the union can avoid liability if the action is repudiated by the principal executive committee, president or general secretary.

9 *Limits on damages against unions.* The upper limits on damages awarded against a union in a single set of legal proceedings for unlawful industrial action are:

where the union has fewer than 5,000 members	£10,000
5,000 - 24,999 members	£50,000
25,000 - 99,999 members	£125,000
100,000 or more members	£250,000

For the dismissal of striking employees or those taking other industrial action, see Chapter 10.

Index

Topic	*Page*